This book
belongs to

Escher H.

from
chad
to Escher
2006

BUGS

The Encyclopedia of Creepy-Crawlies

This book was created by Quartz Editions for Zigzag Publishing,
an imprint of Quadrillion Publishing Ltd.,
Woolsack Way, Godalming, Surrey GU7 1XW, U.K.

Consultant: Matthew Robertson
General Editor: Tamara Green
Designer: Marilyn Franks
Illustrator: Tony Gibbons
Additional illustrations: Clare Heronneau and Neil Lloyd
Cover Design by Triggerfish

This edition published in 1998 in the U.S.
by SMITHMARK Publishers,
a division of U.S. Media Holdings, Inc.,
115 West 18th Street, New York,
NY 10011.

SMITHMARK books are available for bulk
purchase for sales promotion and premium use.
For details write or call the manager of special sales,
SMITHMARK Publishers, 115 West 18th Street,
New York, NY 10011.

ISBN: 0-7651-0935-2

Ref. No. 8603

10 9 8 7 6 5 4 3 2 1

Library of Congress Catalog Card Number: 98-60909

Printed in Hong Kong by Midas Printing Ltd

BUGS

The Encyclopedia of Creepy-Crawlies

SMITHMARK

Contents

Introduction

Welcome to this magnificently illustrated junior encyclopedia of bugs! We hope you will enjoy dipping into its many colorful pages, and discovering a whole wealth of information about the wonderful miniature world of insects and other creepy-crawlies.

You could be in for some surprises. Did you know, for instance, that the ordinary housefly can beat its wings at up to 200 times per second; that some types of male mosquitoes will perform an intricate dance to attract a female prior to mating; that some bugs change form entirely, not once but twice, before becoming mature, in a process known as complete metamorphosis; and that cockroaches – if they get into your home – may nibble not only at your left-overs but also possibly at your sneakers, too?

With the aid of this volume, compiled with the assistance of a highly respected British entomologist, *you*, too, could soon become an expert on bugs! We invite you now to read on...

In the air

How many bugs can you think of that can fly? Even if you can name as many as ten, there may still be some that are entirely new to you in the section that follows – the wonderful doodlebug, perhaps.

You are probably familiar with wasps. Maybe you have even been unlucky enough to be stung by one. But did you know that there are in fact many kinds of wasps – some of them living a solitary existence, others dwelling in communities that may have several thousand in all?

Other types of flying bugs will attack, too, not just if annoyed but if given half a chance. The tsetse fly, for example, will bite and inject its saliva into the skin of an animal – us, too – thereby sometimes passing on diseases that may be deadly if untreated. The ordinary bluebottle can be harmful as well, spreading germs of all kinds if allowed to land on your food. Locusts are also unpopular bugs, since they cause terrible devastation to crops. In fact, they were one of the ten dreadful plagues sent to the ancient Egyptians, according to biblical account.

There are, however, many winged beauties – such as butterflies, ladybugs and grasshoppers – that provide a veritable visual, and sometimes auditory treat with their pleasing colors and patterns, or tuneful song. But do you know how butterflies reproduce, how a cicada sings, or how a housefly manages to walk upside-down on the ceiling? How do bees make honey? And did you know that a flying bug's wings are powered not by muscles in the wings themselves but by muscles inside their thorax? Many more intriguing mysteries about the world of flying bugs are about to be revealed.

Flies

There are, in all, about 80,000 different types of flies. Some buzz, some bite, and some spread disease. Among the most familiar is the housefly, a common visitor to our homes in warm weather.

This housefly shown here has, of course, been enlarged a great many times. First, let's take a look at its head. What enormous eyes it has! They are quite different from yours. Humans have just one lens in each eye. But, amazingly, the eyes of a housefly each comprise about 4,000 six-sided lenses. With them, flies can see almost all around themselves, but not far into the distance. They can also recognize a variety of different colors, including ultra-violet light, which is a sort of light that is invisible to us.

On its head, too, are the fly's antennae, or feelers. They are quite small and hang down, while there are other bristles that stick out of its head.

These hairs are sensitive to vibrations, which is why a fly can sense your approach if you try to swat it. As you do so, a wave of air moves ahead of your hand or a flyswatter, causing the hairs to vibrate and warning the fly, so that it has a fraction of a second to escape.

FEEDING TIME
Now take a look at the fly's mouth area. At the front, a long feeding tube, called the proboscis, sticks out. This is used for sucking up liquids, just as you do when you drink with a straw.

World of the fly

- Houseflies, mysteriously, seem to disappear in winter. How, then, do they reappear in such large numbers in summer? They lay lots of eggs which hatch in just a day, reaching the adult stage within 11 days.

Compound eye

Antennae

Proboscis

The housefly cannot digest lumps of solid food, so it mostly takes in fluid. On its proboscis, however, the fly also has mini-teeth that it uses for biting off the tiniest bits of food. These bits are then softened by liquids that the fly can regurgitate.

ON BALANCE

Most flies have a pair of true wings that they use for flight. There is, however, another pair of hind or back wings, known as halteres, which have the job of helping the fly with balance. (In spite of their name, a few types of flies do not have wings at all, however.)

The housefly's six legs are long and slim, and have padded feet that are useful for walking upside-down on ceilings as you will discover when you turn the page.

Houseflies are prolific breeders – so much so that one expert has even estimated that a single pair might have enough offspring to cover the whole of Switzerland to a depth of 49ft (15m), over 6 months, if they all survived to produce further generations of surviving offspring.

Houseflies will not bite, as some other species of flies do; but they are undoubtedly a nuisance in their own right when they come visiting.

FACTFILE

Scientists have been able to estimate that the fastest fly can zoom through the air at the incredible speed of about 25mph (40km/h).

Padded feet

Amazing acrobatics

Among the best acrobats of the insect world, flies perform a range of tricks as a perfectly natural part of their everyday lives.

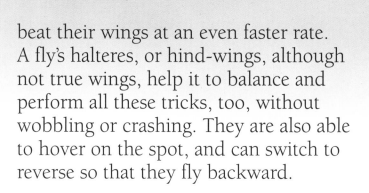

Unless you are a fantasy character like Batman, you would find it impossible to climb up walls or to walk across the ceiling of a room. To the ordinary housefly, however, such acrobatics are no problem at all. So how do they do it?

The secret lies in the sticky pads that they have on the bottom of their feet. These give them a grip on all sorts of surfaces – horizontal or vertical. You may even spot them sometimes stretching out their legs and doing a half-spin in order to land on the ceiling, upside-down.

Flies are also amazingly speedy while in flight and are difficult to catch. Their wings are powered by a system of strong muscles in the thorax. In fact, scientists believe that the ordinary housefly may beat its wings an astonishing 200 times each second! Tiny flies, like mosquitoes and midges, beat their wings at an even faster rate. A fly's halteres, or hind-wings, although not true wings, help it to balance and perform all these tricks, too, without wobbling or crashing. They are also able to hover on the spot, and can switch to reverse so that they fly backward.

World of the fly

- In all, there are nearly 100,000 types of flies, and they can be found almost everywhere on Planet Earth. Many look very different – bluebottles, daddy longlegs, horseflies, midges and mosquitoes, for instance.

UP, UP, AND AWAY

The wings of flies are powered by muscles attached to the walls of the thorax. When the vertical muscles contract, the wings move upward. Then, when longitudinal muscles contract, the wings move downward. A fly's wings are also operated by a system of tiny locks that are released when there is a certain amount of tension. As the tension in the walls of the thorax is released, speed builds up.

All this requires a great deal of energy, so flies constantly seek food to fuel their activity. The food we eat is ideal, but never allow flies near it.

A single housefly can carry over a million bacteria on its legs, body, or proboscis, or may regurgitate part of a previous nasty meal. So never leave food lying around uncovered if flies are around. Houseflies also feed on sewage and may have done so before flying in through a window or door. This means they can carry bacteria that cause disease – food poisoning, or worse.

At meals, don't let flies near your plate, and always empty the kitchen garbage regularly. Great fun to watch at their acrobatics, flies are nevertheless unwanted pests and should be shooed outdoors if they manage to get in.

Birth of a fly

The life cycle of a fly follows a series of remarkable changes during which it develops from an egg to a maggot, and then on to a pupa, before the adult insect finally emerges.

It is usually summertime when greenbottles – a common type of fly – mate. First, a

dead creature, such as the hedgehog in these pictures, will be an ideal spot.

The eggs are tiny – only about the size of the period at the end of this sentence – but there are over 100 of them in total. They do not have a hard shell, like a much larger hen's egg does, for instance, but are soft.

In just a day or so, tiny larvae, which are known as maggots, emerge from the eggs. These maggots will eventually turn into adult greenbottles.

But first the maggots have to feed on the dead hedgehog's body so that

male fly will climb on to a female's back and they stay like this for a while. You have probably seen them do this.

Then, when the male flies off, the female greenbottle is ready to find somewhere suitable to lay her fertilized eggs. A garbage heap or the body of a

they will grow. As yet, they have no visible head, no legs, and no wings.

After about a week, the maggots wriggle their way into soil. Their skin now becomes harder, and they shed it. Once they have done this, each maggot has become what is called a pupa.

Inside each pupa, an adult greenbottle is still developing. It will take about a week, depending on the temperature, for it to emerge from the pupa's shell. It splits the circular cap at one end of the case, using a special part of its head, known as the ptilinum. For a while, the young greenbottle is soft and cannot fly. But it soon hardens and will take to the air. How green and shiny its body is now!

In one season, millions of flies come into existence as a result of the original mating of just one male and one female.

World of the fly

- Spiders, frogs, birds, and a few mammals are all insectivores, preying on flies. But many flies camouflage themselves quite successfully, and will of course fly off very quickly to avoid being caught.

Most flies seem to disappear when winter comes to countries that have a cold season, or are found only in heated buildings. They survive most easily in the heat; but even in freezing temperatures, a few stay alive by hibernating, and they may even breed very slowly in winter in fermenting garbage heaps. In parts of the world where it is constantly hot, however, they are a nuisance all year round, and mating is not seasonal.

Daddy longlegs

You have probably often seen daddy longlegs bobbing up and down when at rest, or flying around your electric light, if they happen to get indoors.

No wonder crane flies have been given the amusing nickname of daddy longlegs. It is in honor of their delicate, thread-like limbs. These are, as you can see, quite unlike the legs of most other flies.

You will find them during the summer mostly, in gardens or the countryside. And, if they get indoors, you may notice how attracted they are to electric light.

They often get into houses at night, after spending the day on a wall or hidden between grass stems or under leaves, and they will flap around furiously, trying to find an escape route.

An adult daddy longlegs does not eat or drink much, feeding just on nectar and water. But the growing larva (also known as a leatherjacket) that will turn into a daddy longlegs eats a great amount of plant stems, roots, and grass.

A daddy longlegs' spindly legs trail behind so much that they can easily be caught in a spider's web as they fly past.

They have to beware of such newly-spun traps.

Some types of crane flies – and even their larvae – are carnivorous and may enjoy eating small worms or dragonfly nymphs. Some will also turn cannibalistic and start to eat their own kind.

DELICATE WINGS

There are an enormous number of species of crane flies – about 10,000 in total. Most are delicate and find windy conditions a problem.

FACTFILE

Crane flies do not fly quickly and so may be vulnerable to lots of different predators, which can easily grasp them by their long legs.

Fighting flies

Some types of fly carry bacteria that can spread serious diseases. So we need to do all we can to keep their numbers down.

In the biblical book *Exodus*, there is an account of the ten plagues that afflicted Egypt as a punishment. The fourth of these was a plague of flies. "*The land was corrupted by reason of the swarms of flies.*" These swarms no doubt deposited bacteria on the Egyptians' food and made them ill.

A number of methods have been tried in the attempt to kill flies of various kinds in recent years. Swamps have been drained, for instance, and a special chemical, known as DDT, has been used in the battle against mosquitoes – tiny flies that spread the deadly diseases malaria and yellow fever. But mosquitoes soon became immune to the effect of DDT. Worse still, many fish, birds and mammals were affected by it, so other insecticides were used. But some flies have managed to become resistant to the effects of these insecticides, too.

Scientists have even tried to eliminate some types of flies by sterilizing the males so that they cannot fertilize the females. But flies are hardy. In any event, if all flies were wiped out, many birds would starve and some flowers would not become pollinated so easily. Flies, you see, have their uses, too.

FACTFILE

There are some sorts of flies that live only on certain types of plants and will nibble at them – the carrot fly, for example.

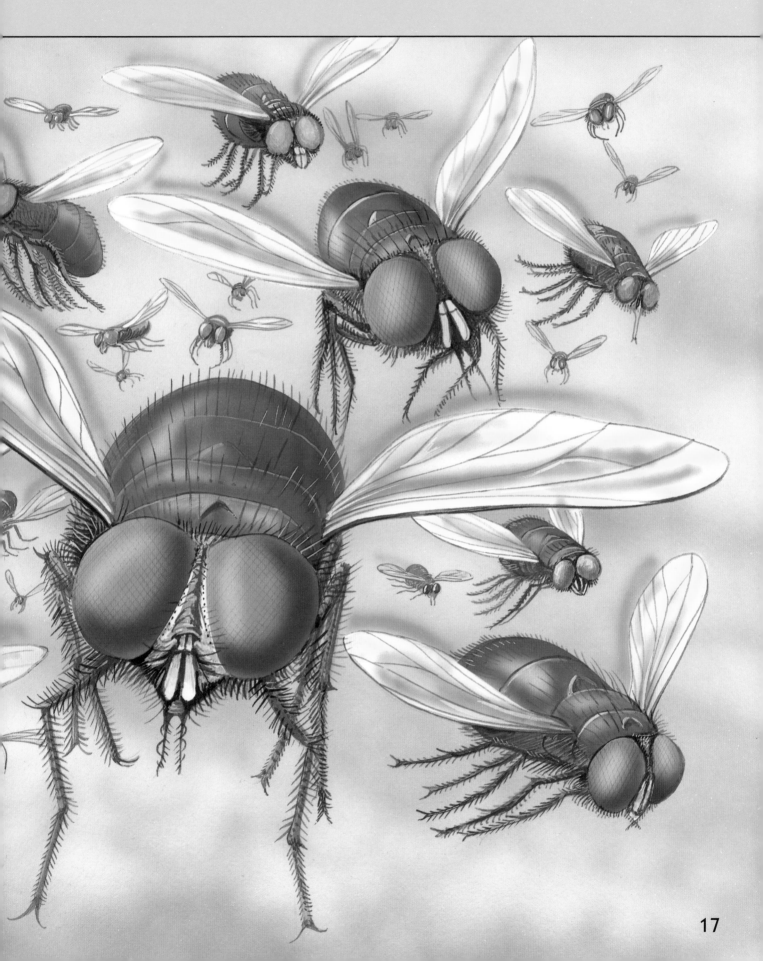

Tsetse flies

Houseflies are bad enough, with the germs they can spread. But other types of flies can actually kill you if they bite and treatment is delayed.

Two of our most deadly insect enemies are shown *opposite* – tsetse flies that are native to Africa and spreaders of many serious diseases, particularly one called sleeping sickness.

Also known by the scientific name *Glossina*, tsetse flies love to feed on blood. Both sexes will bite your skin, given half a chance, in order to get at some of your blood. As a result, the nasty parasites that they carry can enter your bloodstream, and may cause fever, swelling, coma, and even death.

As you can see in this picture, tsetse flies look completely different from the ordinary housefly. Tsetse flies are usually dark and have a mixture of brown and cream spots, stripes and other markings. They are little bigger than houseflies and fold their wings, one over the other, so that these look like the blades of a closed pair of scissors when they are resting.

LIVE BIRTH

Houseflies, as you discovered earlier in this book, lay eggs; but tsetse flies do not. Instead, they are viviparous. This means that, after mating, females give birth to live larvae that then proceed to burrow into the soil.

In the soil, before they become adults, each larva first changes into a pupa. During this stage, its body develops to maturity. It is a process that takes about four weeks.

Each female tsetse fly does not produce more than about 12 larvae during her lifetime. Both males and females also have short lifespans – only about six months in all.

One of the two tsetse flies that you can see enlarged here is extremely fat with a bulging red abdomen because it has just sucked up its own weight in blood. That will give you an idea of how terribly greedy it is! Tsetse flies feed on the blood of mammals, including humans, birds and reptiles, and from a living host, unlike most other types of flies. Even crocodiles cannot escape their attack, despite their tough skin!

World of the fly

- In an attempt to eradicate the tsetse fly, some are raised in laboratories and sterilized. They are then released where sleeping sickness is endemic, so that the females will not produce fertilized eggs and numbers will be reduced.

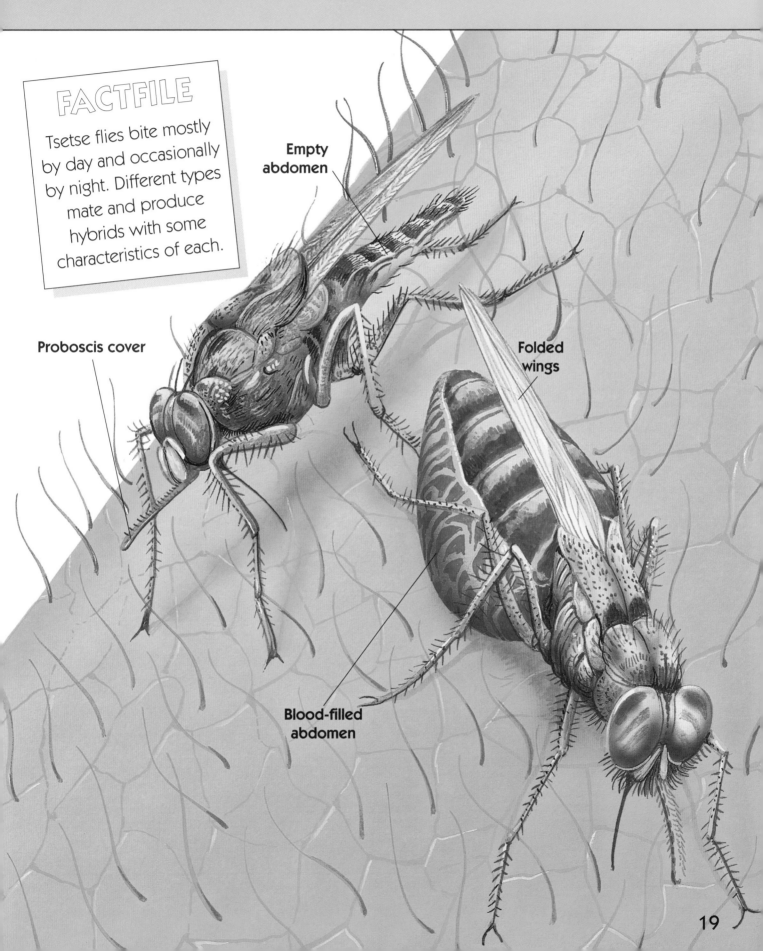

Empty abdomen

Proboscis cover

Folded wings

Blood-filled abdomen

Four more flies

Midges, horse flies, dance flies, and hover flies all have their own distinctive appearances and behavior patterns.

When you are outside in warm weather, perhaps on a picnic, you may be annoyed by a swarm of tiny flies known as midges. These flies can be found all over the planet and, in some regions of the world, are called 'no-seeums' because they are so small. You can see one, however, greatly enlarged in the illustration on the *right*.

OUT FOR BLOOD

You may also have noticed midges on a summer evening, hovering in groups of several hundred over water. Some will even attack the larger mosquitoes to suck blood or they may damage crops, such as wheat.

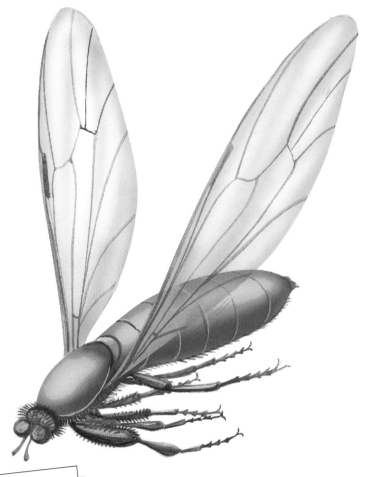

FACTFILE

It is hard to catch a fly because its eyes have many lenses and it can spot the slightest movement, even from behind.

PAINFUL BITES

Other flies bite, too, and the horse fly, *bottom left*, is just one example. Despite its name, it not only attacks horses, but also humans, and can deliver a painful bite with its sharp proboscis. As with mosquitoes, it is the female horse flies that will bite you for your blood. There are about 3,000 known species of horseflies; and the males will often swarm prior to mating. Both males and females will also visit flowers to feed on nectar and, in doing so, pollinate the plants.

World of the fly

- Some types of flies produce larvae that feed on aphids. Others have larvae that feed on the blood of frogs, while some larvae are purely vegetarian.

FLOATING ON AIR

Hover flies, as their name suggests, tend to hover in the air. You will also see them glide sideways, forward or backward, upward or downward. As you can see *below*, they look more like bees or wasps than true flies. They have boldly patterned bodies and, like horse flies, make themselves useful by pollinating flowers. What big eyes they have! Listen for their song, too, as they buzz after settling.

GENEROUS GIVERS

Dance flies, like the ones *above*, seen mating, get their name from the way the males dance as part of their courtship behavior. This dance is frequently seen during summer in temperate regions. The males also bring gifts – usually another sort of fly – to the females which the females eat while mating.

But the males are greedy and often snatch it away from one female to give to another female before mating with *her*! Some will even kill their own species to give to a female, which is why they are also known as assassin flies. They have a habit of pouncing on their prey, and look a lot like robber flies, with powerful, bristly, grasping legs, but more rounded heads.

Ladybugs

These small and brightly colored creatures can be found in many gardens during the summer months. They are cute to look at, but some give out a nasty smell. Nevertheless, they have a very useful role to play when it comes to horticulture.

Ladybugs are probably everyone's favorite type of beetle. They seem quite tame, and you can often tempt them onto your finger. What is more, according to legend, if a ladybug lands on you, good luck follows.

Your garden will certainly have good fortune if ladybugs choose to live there. This is because aphids such as greenfly and blackfly – which destroy plants – are the ladybug's favourite meal. In fact, as soon as a ladybug larva hatches from its egg, it is able to munch its way through up to thirty of these garden pests a day.

You can recognize a ladybug by its red body and bold black spots. This is the most common type, and is known as "the seven-spot ladybug."

FACTFILE

In its lifetime, a single ladybug may gobble down as many as several thousand greenflies – clearly a gardener's friend!

The seven-spot ladybug also likes to feast on the young larvae of the dreaded Colorado beetle. Farmers who grow potatoes, therefore, often make an effort to bring in lots of ladybugs to save their crops.

The ladybug larva is dull and knobby, but is still a favorite meal for birds. However, birds will think twice about dining on an *adult* ladybug. The ladybug has yellow blood, which it squirts out from joints in its knees when attacked. It hopes the bird – or any other predator – will find the meal so vile that it will spit it out.

MULTI-COLORED

Not all ladybugs are red with black spots, however. Some are black with red spots, or yellow with black spots. You may even be lucky enough to spy a white ladybug. This is a very young adult. Its spots and body color take several hours to appear after it has emerged.

Ladybugs may come indoors in winter, for both warmth and rest. Do not disturb them. They will wake up and fly outside again when spring arrives.

Mosquitoes

The word mosquito comes from Spanish and simply means "little fly." But these tiny creatures can be a terrible nuisance in spite of their size, and may spread disease.

If you look at a mosquito under a microscope, you can see that the 0.3in (8mm)-long insect, like most flies, has two huge orbs for eyes. These contain hundreds of tiny lenses that give it excellent eyesight. You will also be able to see the two long antennae, or feelers, at the front of its head. A male's antennae, as shown here, are covered with thousands of hairs and look like feathers, while a female has long, slender antennae. Mosquitoes use these to feel their way along, and also to sense if a female is nearby.

If you turn to page 31, you can see a female mosquito.

FACTFILE

If a female mosquito feeds on the blood of a human with yellow fever, it can pass on the disease to the next person it bites.

Only the female will suck blood, and it uses needle-sharp spikes on its head to feed on the blood of any passing animals – birds and humans, too.

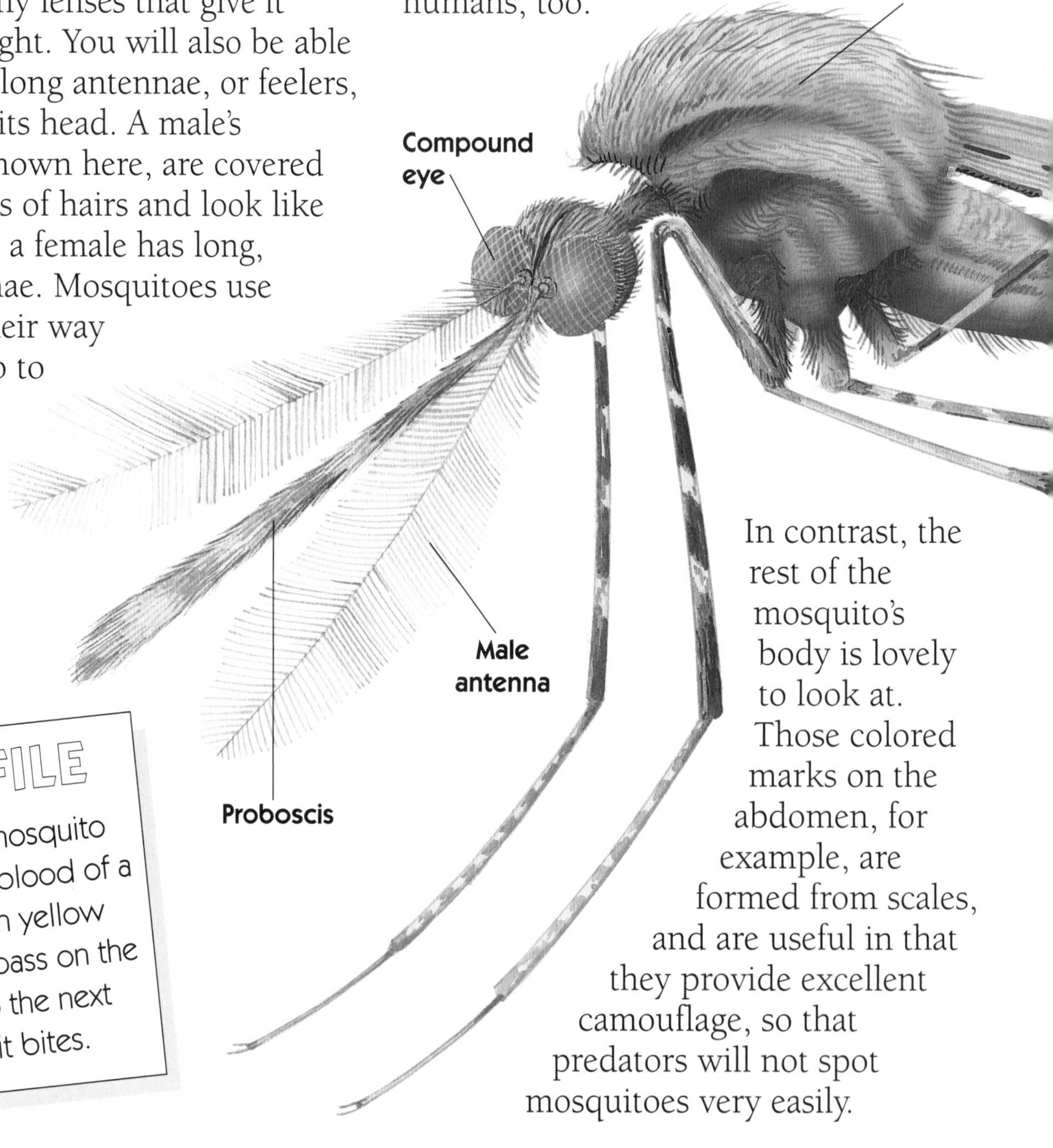

Thorax
Compound eye
Male antenna
Proboscis

In contrast, the rest of the mosquito's body is lovely to look at. Those colored marks on the abdomen, for example, are formed from scales, and are useful in that they provide excellent camouflage, so that predators will not spot mosquitoes very easily.

World of the mosquito

- A mosquito's antennae are so extremely sensitive to sound waves that they take on the function of ears, which are otherwise absent in the insect.

Wings

Abdomen

Mosquitoes come in many colors. Some are plain brown, to merge against a background of tree-bark, while others have jazzy black-and-white stripes that will make them almost invisible in a woodland's dappled shade.

SHIMMERING WINGS

The mosquito is called a "true" fly because it has two wings. These wings also have scales, which shimmer in sunlight. So transparent that you can see right through them, they are made from membranes that are divided up like stained-glass windows by black, thread-like veins.

The mosquito can also crawl around on its six long, spidery legs. These allow it to make a soft and silent landing on animals or humans, who will probably be unaware that a female mosquito is there or who will merely feel the slightest tickle – until it bites, of course!

CREATURES OF THE NIGHT

Mosquitoes love the night and, unlike other flies, most will shun sunlight and other bright light. They can be crafty creatures, too. One type will even hover over a certain type of ant carrying honeydew, which it will steal right out of the ant's mouth.

Noisy biters

A common heat-loving insect, the mosquito often announces its presence by buzzing and a female may give a particularly nasty bite.

If you ever happen to be out by a pond on a warm summer's evening and start to hear some buzzing, the chances are you will soon spot a swarm of tiny flies hovering over the water.

What an amazing sight! But remember not to get too close. The females might attack and bite, sucking up a little of your blood. Most of them will be males, as a rule, however. They do not suck blood, preferring to feed on sugary liquids, such as nectar. The males do not buzz, either; so all that loud noise is coming from females.

MATING GAMES

You would not think that just a few insects could make so much noise, but mosquito wings beat the air at an amazing 500 beats every second. In fact, you may notice that the males sometimes go quite wild.

Such commotion is a mating game. Some types of male mosquitoes even swarm in a kind of dance in order to attract the females.

If they are interested in mating, the female mosquitoes will not be looking for a person to bite – not yet. But, later, they are sure to want a blood-meal before they lay their eggs because of the protein it provides – so that is the time to avoid them.

When a female mosquito is hungry for blood, she will land on her victim's skin. The outer covering of her mouthparts will then slide back to reveal the piercing mandibles, which are also known as stylets.

World of the mosquito

- Amazingly, there may be more than 2,400 different species of mosquitoes which inhabit the majority of countries throughout the world.

Serrated-edged maxillae now cut through the skin and stab the unlucky bird, rabbit, cow, snake, or human. All may be bitten in this way, and experience intense irritation.

27

Birth of a mosquito

All mosquitoes begin their life in water, and different species have different ways of hatching.

Once they have mated, female mosquitoes will automatically fly to almost anywhere that has one or two inches (a few centimeters) of water. Ponds or puddles, marshpools or ditches – all are ideal.

But if there happens to be no natural stretch of water nearby, then anything – such as water butts, or small puddles in old tin cans – will do just as well. Mosquitoes are not very fussy about their breeding grounds.

Most types of female mosquitoes need a blood-meal before they lay their eggs. One type of mosquito, known as the culicine mosquito, lays up to three hundred eggs, which all stick together and float on the surface of the water.

At this stage, they look like a tiny raft that is only about 0.25in (5mm) long, as seen enlarged *below*.

Anopheline mosquitoes, however, lay only about 30 single eggs, each with an outer shell that traps air inside and acts as a tiny float.

This is to keep the eggs from sinking to the bottom of the water.

After a few days, each individual larva hatches out through a special trapdoor at the bottom of the egg, and wriggles to the surface.

World of the mosquito

- Mosquito larvae feed on tiny floating organisms, known as algae and protozoa. Some will only survive in oxygenated water.

Culicine larvae have a tube at their tail-end to suck up air, and they hang upside down in a row, like washing on a line, as shown *below*.

Anopheline larvae, however, have two

the surface. Before long, they enter a further stage of their development and change completely.

Adult mosquitoes take less than a week to emerge from the pupae, without even getting wet! Then they shake their wings and are ready to fly.

trumpet-like tubes on their heads, and they lie flat under the water to breathe.

After about three weeks, they develop into pupae. These are curved, just like a comma, and also wriggle around under

Some mosquitoes hibernate in winter; but in very hot climates, when there is drought, they may rest in a process known as aestivation. Once the rains come, they will be on the wing again.

Blood meats

In spite of attempts to wipe them out, our hard-fought war against mosquitoes still continues.

Lots of flies like the light – but not most mosquitoes! They are mostly nocturnal creatures and far prefer to hide until it becomes dark.

In hot countries, where mosquitoes tend to be the malaria-carrying kind, many people will put up a special sort of net around their beds to protect them from mosquito bites while they sleep, as in the picture *below*.

Burning a bright light all night also helps to keep them away. But not all mosquitoes come out at night. Forest mosquitoes of some species are diurnal – which means they come out during the day. They prefer the warmth of the sun to the cold of the night. These are more likely to attack at sunrise and sunset, seeking a blood-meal after they wake, and again before they rest.

KILLER DISEASE

Every year, there are about 250 million cases of malaria reported worldwide, and some two million people die from it. Half of these are children who live in poor countries, where treatment can be hard to get.

In the picture *opposite*, enlarged several thousand times under a microscope, you can see how two malaria parasites (colored by the artist in blue and pink) have invaded a red blood cell after a bite from a malaria-carrying mosquito, like the one shown *bottom right*.

Mosquitoes suck up malaria germs when biting someone who already has malaria. These germs then breed inside the mosquitoes and infect their saliva.

World of the mosquito

- A female mosquito may attack as many as 18 victims in an hour, sucking their blood and possibly passing on disease from one to another.

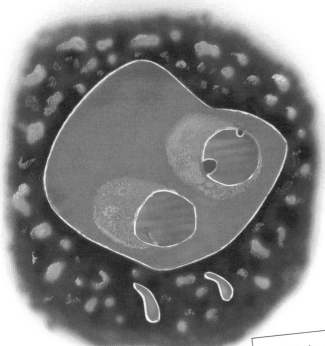

You will not get malaria every time you are bitten by a mosquito. Only one type can infect you, and it lives mainly in tropical regions, such as some Mediterranean countries, Southeast Asia, Africa, and South America.

Once, many victims of malaria were treated with a medicine known as quinine. If you travel today to a country where it is possible to catch malaria, you can take modern drugs before you go, when you are there, and when you come back, to prevent the disease. Your doctor can advise about this. As yet, there is no vaccine to protect us entirely from malaria. But scientists are still hoping to develop one.

When the mosquitoes next need a blood-meal, they pierce their new victim's skin and inject the infected saliva. The unfortunate victim then becomes very ill.

Imagine being in an unbearably hot room but feeling freezing cold. Then, suddenly, you can't stand the heat as your temperature soars to over 105°F (40°C). Your whole body is shaking, and your head aches. You'd feel like this if you had malaria. But, fortunately, there are drugs that will usually cure an attack if administered promptly. Even so, many people still die from malaria – one of the world's biggest killers.

FACTFILE

It was not until 1897 that the scientist Ronald Ross proved that people can catch malaria directly from mosquitoes.

Butterflies

Butterflies are such attractive creatures that it is hard to believe they start their lives as prickly, creepy-crawly caterpillars and only later transform to become winged beauties like this birdwing butterfly.

Butterflies (and their close relatives, the moths) belong to a group of insects that scientists call *Lepidoptera*, a name that means "scaly wings."

In fact, a butterfly's wings are not only lovely but much stronger than they look, so that they can carry their owner right across a continent during migration. Some butterflies even have wings with blood that contains a special chemical to stop them from freezing if they encounter icy weather on the way.

Let's now examine the rest of the butterfly's body. Like other insects, it has three main sections – the head, the thorax and the abdomen. Attached to the thorax are three pairs of legs, each of which is separated into four parts. The first pair of legs is sometimes very weak, and is kept tucked up under the butterfly's head.

A butterfly can see quite well, but its eyes are not nearly as useful as its antennae. These powerful sensors stick out from its head and can detect scents over great distances by means of thousands of tiny holes which act as sophisticated smelling devices.

Scaly wing

Clubbed antennae

FACTFILE

The caterpillars of some types of butterflies secrete a liquid that ants like, so that they live together symbiotically.

Butterflies use their antennae to find both mates and food, and often clean the antennae so that they remain in good working order.

Once it comes to rest on a flower, a butterfly might start feeding on a sweet substance called nectar. To do this, it unrolls its long, tongue-like sucking tube known as a proboscis. This can reach far down into the flower's stem where the nectar is kept.

Amazingly, a butterfly does not rely on

Abdomen

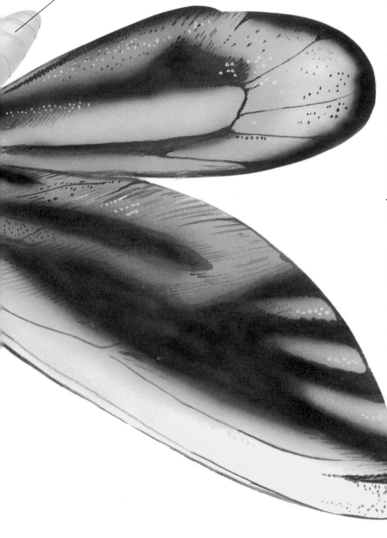

World of the butterfly

- Most types of butterflies have special scent patches on their antennae that they use to sniff out another of their type before mating.

a tongue but can use its feet to taste leaves! Just by feeling the surface of a leaf with its feet, it can tell if it is the right type of leaf on which to lay eggs.

MALE AND FEMALE

Sometimes it is difficult to tell male and female butterflies apart, but there are a large number that have different markings. The male Orange Tip, for instance, has orange tips on its wings, just as the name suggests; but the female has no orange coloration at all.

You can find different species of butterflies all over the world – in fact, there are about 18,000 types in all, and experts are always discovering new ones. Some, however, are becoming very rare, mainly because of the destruction of their habitat – clearing woodland for building, for example – and have even been listed as endangered species. But many rare types are now preserved in butterfly houses, where living insects are encouraged to breed.

BUTTERFLIES

Winged beauties

There are many thousands of species of butterflies, many of them extremely brightly colored, with intricate patterns on their wings.

We feature here four of the world's enormous variety of butterflies. First of all, meet the Monarch, *below*, a North American migrating butterfly. Its markings occur on both sides of the wings and may look pretty, but birds need to beware – its caterpillars and the butterfly itself are very poisonous!

The Long-tailed Figtree butterfly, *below*, can be found in most parts of Africa. Just look at those stunning blue patches on the

reddish wings! The underside of the wings, however, are a plain orange-brown color. There is very little diffference between a male and female Figtree butterfly, except that the female is larger, and has less blue on the hindwings. The underside of both is burnt orange in color; and, as the name suggests, it has a characteristic long tail.

FACTFILE

Most female butterflies will die soon after laying their eggs near a food source for the larvae to feed on when they hatch.

The Cairns Birdwing, illustrated *below*, is found in areas of Southeast Asia and Northern Australia. If you see one with flashes on its green wings, you will know that it is a male of the species. Female Cairns Birdwings are completely different in their coloring: they are basically black with white markings on their wings. These particular butterflies are strong fliers, having a wingspan of about 5in (13cm).

The European Peacock, *above*, has one large eyespot on each wing. These are not real eyes, of course, but patches of color that are used for scaring off an enemy. What a superb built-in way of fooling a predator!

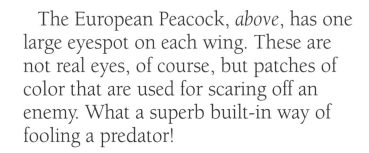

World of the butterfly

- Butterflies are very valuable to plants as pollinators. They carry out this important task as they travel to find the nectar on which they feed.

New generations – 1

When you were first born, you looked just like a smaller version of the child you are now. But that is not true of butterflies.

Before they become fully mature adults, butterflies will go through three main stages and will look entirely different during each one, as you can see in this sequence of pictures, which is continued over the following two pages. The complete cycle from egg to adult butterfly involves distinct physical changes, and this is known as metamorphosis.

After mating with a male, the female will find a suitable spot to lay her eggs. You can see them on a leaf, *below*. There may be just two or three, or many more: this varies from one type of butterfly to another.

The female, however, usually abandons her eggs, sometimes dying very soon afterwards. Inside, meanwhile, the larvae are developing rapidly, and they can sometimes even be observed moving around, so thin is the outer coating of the egg.

World of the butterfly

- Butterflies lay their eggs singly or in clusters, and attach them to the upper or lower surface of leaves with a sticky secretion made in their own bodies.

Two or three weeks later, the larvae hatch and proceed to eat their eggshells. This meal of eggshells provides the larvae with the vital nutrition they need as they start the most important feeding stage of their lifecycle – that of the caterpillar.

Caterpillars, such as those you

can see on the leaves *above*, however, still look nothing at all like the most beautiful creatures they will eventually become. Before that happens, they will take on a further, very different form, as revealed *on the next page*.

New generations – 2

How amazing it is that a caterpillar can change into the strangely shaped immobile creature below!

Something most extraordinary will happen after the caterpillar has molted four or five times. But first the caterpillar must find itself a quiet place, well away from the path of its enemies. Sometimes, this may mean hiding in a tree, hollowing out a space for itself under the ground, or resting unobtrusively on a leaf.

World of the butterfly

- Some pupae are suspended from a surface; others may be wrapped in a cocoon of plant matter, which may be above or below ground.

The pupa does not move around like a caterpillar but remains fairly still. The pupae of some butterflies are shaped like twigs

A new stage is now about to start.
Suddenly the caterpillar's skin begins to split, falling away from its body to reveal what is called a pupa or chrysalis.

or leaves. They are hard to spot, so they stand a better chance of survival.

After a couple of weeks, or even as long as a few months, depending on the species, the pupa reaches maturity. Some species have a covering that is almost transparent, so that the butterfly inside can be seen even before it splits for the adult to free itself. This usually happens in the morning. The head tends to come out first, before the body. But it is not easy when you

At last, after quite a struggle for some pupae, the adult butterfly stretches its crumpled wings and flies off. Metamorphosis is now complete.

consider that some pupae will be underground, while others are inside coverings made from vegetable matter.

Attracting butterflies

Even if you live in an apartment and have no garden, you can still study caterpillars and watch the process of metamorphosis.

If you are lucky enough to have a garden but butterflies do not seem to visit it very often, you might like to try some ways of attracting them.

A first step is to make sure the garden will appeal to female butterflies that are looking for a place to lay their eggs. Butterflies like to lay their eggs on certain plants: nettles, thistles and clover seem to be particular favorites. Plant some in a sunny corner of your garden and, come summer, you can begin to look out for a whole assortment of colorful visitors.

Butterflies also like to feed on the nectar in the flowers of particular plants. Indeed, the buddleia in the picture *opposite* is often called the "butterfly bush" because they love its nectar and are attracted to it.

Even if you do not have a garden, you might like to study caterpillars, which will become butterflies as described on pages 36-39. You can keep your caterpillars in plastic boxes with air holes. But do not put too many in one box. If you find that they become cannibalistic and eat each other, keep them individually.

Each day, supply your caterpillars with fresh plant food. Line the box with blotting paper, so that it is easier to clean out. As the caterpillars grow, they will need larger boxes and twigs on which to pupate. Once at the pupa stage, however, they no longer need food. When a butterfly emerges and its wings have dried out, it can be released at the spot where you found the original caterpillar and fly free at last.

NATURAL HABITATS

Conservationists who work to save the world's plant and animal life believe we could save many butterfly species by taking care of their natural habitats and by setting up special butterfly reserves in various parts of the world. What a wonderful way to ensure that future generations of these exquisite creatures continue to brighten up our planet!

World of the butterfly

- South American Indians believe that if you tie a picture of a butterfly to the bedpost at night, you will be sure to have sweet dreams.

- According to another piece of folklore, if a butterfly comes into your house, there will be a wedding in the family in the near future.

Staying alive

Butterflies can be found almost all over the world, in a huge number of varieties. Some travel long distances to other countries.

When autumn reaches southeastern Canada, prior to winters with shiveringly low temperatures, the Monarch butterfly population instinctively decides to leave for warmer territory. They band together in huge flocks and fly down to California and even southern Mexico.

The journey might take them about three months; but, by then, they will have covered a distance of around 2,500 miles (4,000km).

Once they arrive, they get down to mating and will soon die. Their offspring then instinctively return to Canada in time for the warmer weather.

RARE SPECIES

Some butterflies are found only in particular parts of the globe; and, in many cases, conservationists report that their numbers are seriously dwindling. The rarest (and largest) butterfly of all, for instance, is thought to be the Queen Alexandra's birdwing. It is found in only one part of Papua New Guinea, and became increasingly rare as the rain forest was cleared for farming. With a wingspan of 12in (30cm), it is now listed as an endangered species and protected by international law.

FACTFILE

In all, there are about 170,000 species of *Lepidoptera* that have been discovered so far. Around 90 percent of these are moths.

Sadly, several other types of butterflies are also at risk or have even disappeared altogether. Among them is the Large Blue, which was native to Great Britain and is almost, if not completely, extinct by now. This happened because the caterpillars of the Large Blue used to feed on the grubs and eggs of red ants. But these ants stopped nesting in the grass where it either became very overgrown or had been dug up by farmers for their crops.

However, new species of butterflies may even evolve as a result of co-existence with certain plants. In a jungle, for instance, a so-called Heliconid butterfly lays its eggs on a passion flower. The larvae feed and take in poisons, making them distasteful to birds. New types of passion flower then evolve, producing new poisons in the attempt to deter the butterflies. New butterflies, able to cope with the poison of a particular sort of passion flower, also evolve.

Some butterfly collectors will pay high sums of money for the rarest of specimens. One endangered butterfly specimen was even bought for $1,785.00 (over one thousand pounds sterling). We must do all we can to make certain that these beautiful creatures survive in all their many varieties and in their natural environments.

World of the butterfly

- Some butterflies are particularly successful at avoiding predators because their coloring provides good camouflage. Many even have see-through wings.

- Whereas *we* may see a yellow butterfly, some insects can see the same butterfly only in shades of gray.

Moths

How, and where, do moths mate? And how is the next generation born? Study the next four pages to find out all about their life cycle.

Moths often mate while in flight, but they can also do so when resting. Then, once the female has laid her eggs near a food source, they are abandoned, in the same way that the female butterfly will always abandon hers.

The eggs vary a great deal in shape and coloring; but they soon open and the larvae, or caterillars, emerge. This is the first stage in this insect's complete metamorphosis.

Caterpillars do very little with their time except eat furiously. Some are hairy; others look just like twigs; and many have heads that, like the heads of tortoises, can be drawn back in.

Never touch a hairy caterpillar! It may secrete a fluid that stings, and this can have an uncomfortable effect even after it has just died.

In general, caterpillars have very sharp jaws – ideal for grabbing and chewing food. Their bodies have several segments, some with appendages

World of the moth

- Female moths release chemicals known as pheromones. The scent lures the males, and they, too, may also secrete substances that excite the females.

known as prolegs but that are not really legs at all. Nevertheless, they still help caterpillars move along. Attached to the prolegs are tiny suckers and small hooks that help them to balance. The silk threads they emit from their mouths are also useful, in case they fall and need something to help them climb back up again.

Caterpillars will molt several times, casting off their old skin and replacing it with a new covering, which may be a slightly different color.

The old skin may even be eaten by the caterpillar; but it will not devour the hard part that formerly covered its head, because this would be difficult to digest.

WHAT A FEAST!

The caterpillar *below* has been greatly enlarged for clarity, and is the larva of an American Hawkmoth. This larva is also known as a hornworm because of the spike at its rear end. It is a pest of the tomato plant and a nuisance to farmers. Turn the page now and discover all about the next stages in the metamorphosis from a caterpillar to a moth.

FACTFILE

Many moth larvae feed only at night. Some will eat a wide variety of leaves, but others are more particular and like only one kind.

Metamorphosis

The strangely shaped form *below*, is a pupa, or chrysalis – the extraordinary next stage in the metamorphosis of a caterpillar to a moth, like the one shown *far right*.

Having discarded their final skin in a last molt, some moth caterpillars will wriggle to the ground, where they will burrow and prepare to pupate, transforming into a pupa, also known as a chrysalis. Other caterpillars, however, may spin a cocoon while resting either on a tree or plant, or on the ground.

Pupation is no easy process. Indeed, the caterpillar may have to twist itself for a long time in order to get free of its final covering.

Whereas caterpillars move and feed extremely greedily, during the moth's next stage, a pupa will remain almost completely immobile.

Pupae come in many shapes, sizes, and colors. The one shown here belongs to an American Hawkmoth, like the caterpillar on the previous page. It closely resembles a lamp with a handle. The handle part holds this moth's developing proboscis, which it needs for feeding. (Some moths, however, do not have a proboscis, and never feed at all after the greedy larval (caterpillar) stage of their lives.)

FACTFILE

Do not try this yourself, but some Australian aboriginals can identify non-poisonous moth grubs and eat them, raw or roasted.

SILK PRODUCTION

Many thousands of years ago, the Chinese discovered that a certain caterpillar's silk could be woven into textiles for garments or furnishings. Later, silk production was introduced to Greece, the Arab world, Sicily, and elsewhere in Europe, too. But because the manufacturing process involves killing the pupa (or chrysalis) to preserve its silk, many people now regard silk production as cruel and object to wearing it.

It is, however, a very beautiful fabric that feels soft to the touch.

entirely on camouflage for protection from predators. Its wings are small at first, but it will pump up more fluid from its body, so that the wings soon expand.

WASTE DISPOSAL

While waiting for its wings to dry, the new moth must eliminate from its system all the waste that it did not expel as a pupa. This waste is known as its meconium. A new Hawkmoth, like the one shown here, has just been born and is an entirely different in appearance from both the caterpillar and pupa that it once was.

SOFTENING UP

The length of time it takes for the pupa to reach maturity varies according to the species of moth. When it is ready, it will secrete a fluid that softens the cocoon so that it can be forced open by the emerging insect. At this stage, the moth is known as an imago, and is highly vulnerable since, as it cannot fly yet, it has to rely

More about moths

Butterflies and moths both belong to an insect group known as the *Lepidoptera*. But how can you distinguish between them?

One of the principal ways to tell the difference between a moth and a butterfly is to look at how they hold their wings when they are resting. Butterflies usually have their wings upright and together, whereas moths tend to have them lying flat.

Butterflies also usually fly during the day, whereas most moths like to fly at night. But there are some further differences. Butterflies generally have clubbed antennae, but the antennae of moths may be just plain or even furry. Moths also mostly have thicker and hairier bodies. There are a great many more species of moths than of butterflies, too.

Like the example shown *top left* – the huge Hercules moth from New Guinea and parts of Australia – moths are usually less colorful than butterflies; but this is not always the case. In fact, with some moths, bright coloring is often a

World of the moth

• Moths are greatly attracted to light when they fly at night. This is why you may often see them fluttering madly around an electric light if they happen to come indoors.

warning to predators that they are poisonous.

Among these colorful moths is the example shown *top right*, from Southeast Asia. In essence, its coloring signals: *Stay away*!

There is also one type of Hawkmoth that closely resembles a bee which clearly must be an advantage in warning off predators.

Another flamboyant species is the Madagascan Sunset moth, *right*. Often mistaken for a type of Swallowtail butterfly because of its wing shape, it gets its name from the sunset-like patches on its lower wings.

FACTFILE

One of the fastest flying insects is the Hummingbird Hawkmoth, which may reach a speed of 43mph (70km/h).

Enemy attack

Moths have many enemies that will chase them for a meal – among them, bats. How do they succeed at this after nightfall, when it is dark?

Bats excel at hovering – a skill that enables them to pick off their prey from foliage as well as straight from the air. Once caught, the unfortunate victim – in the instance illustrated, a Red Underwing moth from Europe – is carried off to a nearby resting place and devoured. The wings and legs, though, will be discarded: bats do not like these parts of a moth's body.

All this activity takes place under cover of darkness, and is completed in a matter of a few seconds. Who would have thought that a bat, with a brain the size of this

FACTFILE

Some moths can be attacked by types of fungi or by contagious diseases, which may cause them to die prematurely.

World of the moth

- The camouflage markings of moths are usually on the upper surfaces of their wings: remember that they tend to rest with their wings spread. Butterflies, however, tend to have their protective markings on the under-surface of their wings, since they almost always rest with their wings raised.

letter "o", could react so quickly! Although it has poor sight, the bat has one great advantage. It can both move around and pinpoint its prey with extreme precision by means of what is known as echolocation. This operates in the following way.

Although the frequency is far too high for you to hear, ultrasonic sounds are emitted by the bat and these are reflected back from any objects, or creatures, in its flight path. That, quite simply, is how bats avoid bumping into buildings and how they know if a potential meal is nearby.

Some bats even operate such a sensitive echolocation mechanism that they can tell if a tiny caterpillar is sitting on a particular leaf.

At night, camouflage does not offer a great deal of protection to caterpillars or moths. However, moths' eyes have a special reflective layer, so that they shine almost like a cat's eyes do at night. This will, of course, be slightly to their disadvantage, in that they may be more visible than they would otherwise be to some predators.

JAMMING SESSIONS

More positive is the fact that a few types of moths can themselves produce sounds of a very high frequency, and these may actually jam the bat's echolocation mechanism. Certain other moths can even tune in to the ultrasonic sounds made by bats. They do this using hearing organs on their thorax.

Other enemies of moths include frogs, birds, ants, spiders, mantises and hornets; and these will all prey on caterpillars, too. Some insects may even lay their eggs inside caterpillars so that when their own larvae hatch, there is a ready food supply. Particular caterpillars – that of the Elephant Hawkmoth, for example – have a means of terrifying a predator. If this caterpillar rears up, its head resembles that of a snake, dark spots standing out exactly like big, staring snake's eyes. The Cinnabar moth caterpillar will squirt poison at a predator. It needs this protection because it is one of the few day-flying moths. The Puss moth caterpillar, meanwhile, will extend and flash two red filaments at its rear end in order to deter an enemy.

Wasps

When enlarged to this size, the common wasp, *opposite*, looks like an enormous, greedy monster feeding on the nectar it finds so delicious.

Some types of wasps might be confused with bees because of their coloring. But their body shape is in fact very different, as you will see clearly if you turn the page and look at the side view of a hornet, the largest type of social wasps – a type that lives in a colony. Wasps have waists, and bees do not. Bees also tend to be hairier than wasps.

But, like bees, wasps have two very large eyes at the sides of their heads that extend a long way down their faces. These are known as compound eyes and have many thousands of closely-packed lenses, arranged in a honeycomb type of pattern.

Unlike human eyes, which have only one lens, compound eyes enable a wasp to see in many directions simultaneously; and they are very useful for sensing movement, even if they cannot focus sharply. What is more, wasps also have, as you can see here, three more eyes. These are placed at the very tops of their heads, but contain only a single lens, just as yours do.

WITH FEELING

Just look at those large, segmented antennae on the wasp's head! It needs them for smelling and feeling, and they are sensitive to air flow, too. They also act as a form of taste bud. In fact, you may sometimes see a wasp dipping its antennae into things like lemonade or jam. Wasps like sugar and when they do this, they are savoring the sweetness in the food. A wasp's antennae also act as measuring instruments, used to assess the size of each cell when they are building a nest.

THE STINGER

The stinger is also an egg-laying organ through which poison will pass if the wasp is annoyed in some way. So only the females will sting. Disturb a wasp's nest, and there is great risk that many of them will attack.

If, by chance, you *do* get stung, it is a good idea to apply an antihistamine to the area on your skin. Some people are also allergic to wasp stings, and may urgently need to see a doctor if there is a bad reaction. Steer as clear of them as you can; and do not panic if one happens to land on you – this will only make it angry. Keep calm, and chances are it will just fly away, if you are patient.

FACTFILE

Wasps can find their nest if they fly off in search of prey; but if it is moved even slightly, they are usually totally confused.

World of the wasp

- Many queen wasps will hibernate for several months during the winter in harsh climates.

- Wasps have biting mouthparts that are useful for cutting up food and building a nest.

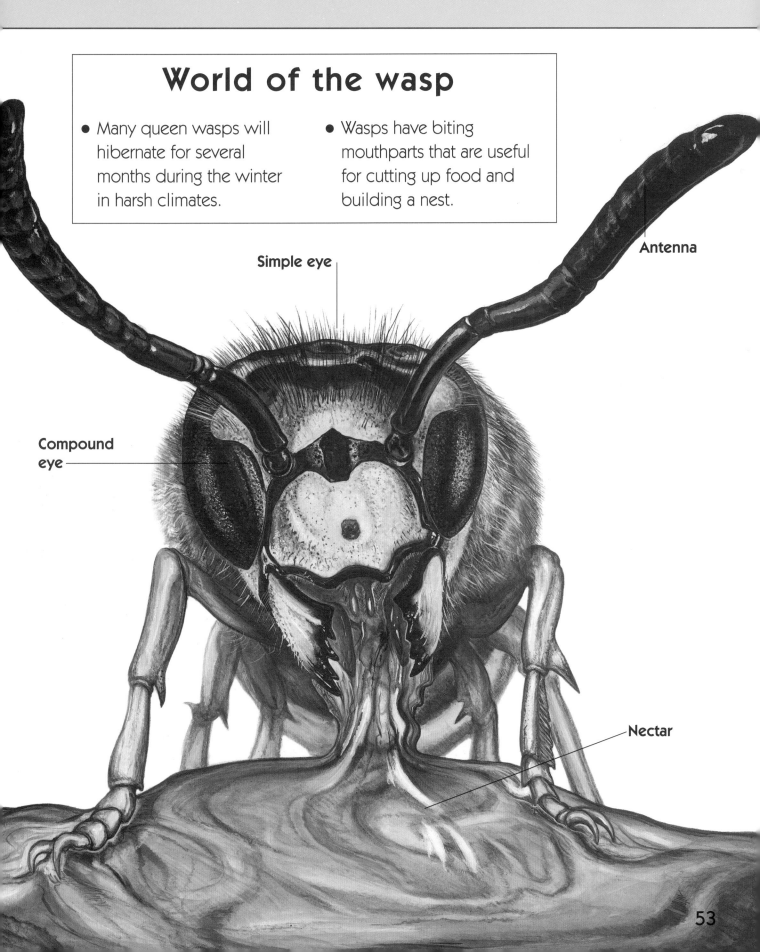

Simple eye

Antenna

Compound eye

Nectar

The hornet

Large members of the wasp family, hornets have bright yellow-orange and brown coloring, and are also known as yellow jackets.

The extremely vibrant stripes of a hornet certainly go a long way toward warning possible prey that they may be out for the kill.

They can be found throughout Europe, North Africa, Asia, and North America, and thrive on other insects, and any sweet food that they come across. They may even attack other wasps and bees, too, such is their size and greedy nature. The robber fly, known to be vicious, is also frequently defeated by the highly aggressive killer hornet.

Intriguingly, hornets are mimicked by certain other insects, including some kinds of flies that may breed in their nests.

This mimicry gives the insect a certain degree of protection.

Skilled nest-builders, they make their many-chambered homes from wood, which they chew into a papery form. The nest is usually begun in spring by the hornet queen, who will have mated with the drones (males). Only the queen is able to produce eggs.

Abdomen

Sting

FACTFILE

Hornets will sting you only if they feel threatened. So if one approaches you, it is best not to swat it but to ignore it.

These soon hatch into larvae, and will be fed by the female workers until mature. Come autumn, most hornets die. But new queens will hibernate and manage to get through the winter. Then, come spring, new nests will be built, and so the cycle continues.

Only the females and queens are able to sting, and will do so in order to paralyse their prey or to kill them outright.

The sting itself is straight, unlike a bee's; and hornets, like all wasps, are able to sting repeatedly, whereas most bees' stings – apart from the queen's – are for one-time use only. Yet, in spite of their large size, hornets are, in fact, less likely to sting than smaller wasps.

After catching their prey – and, for this, their large compound eyes and long antennae, of course, come in very useful – they will usually return to the nest to chew up the meal which will be fed to their larvae.

HORNET INVASION

Sometimes, however, hornets will nest in the roof of a house or other building – a great cause for concern to the occupants, naturally. The noise will be terrific and, of course, insects will often inadvertently get into the house while aiming for the nest. It will therefore be necessary to call in expert pest control officers to cope with the problem and eliminate the colony.

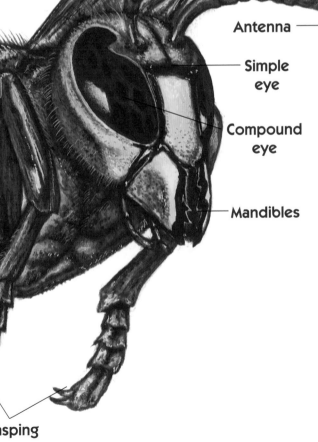

Antenna

Simple eye

Compound eye

Mandibles

Grasping legs

World of the hornet

- The hornet is a social wasp, and lives with many others of its species. Its scientific name is *Vespa crabro*.

Building a nest

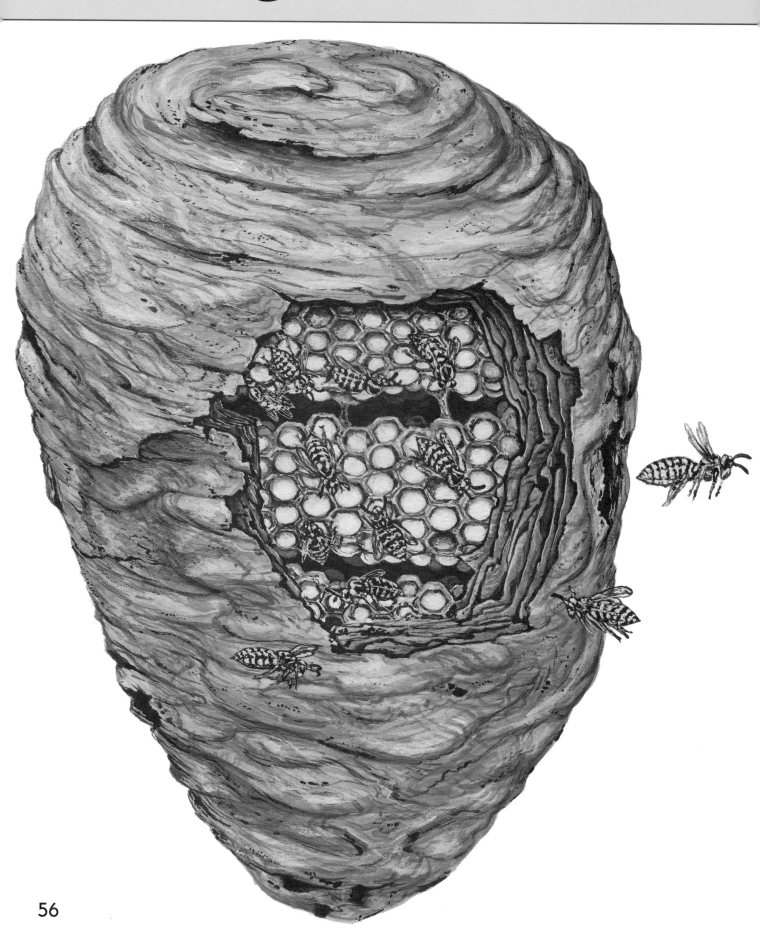

How ingenious some types of wasps are! They even make their own building materials for constructing a nest of many layers.

Take a look at the marvelous wasp's nest, shown *left*. Part of it has been cut away so that you can peek inside, although it would not be safe to do this to any real nest you come across. As you can see, there are a lot of six-sided cells, inside which eggs will be laid. More can be fitted in because they are built hexagonally.

NEW QUEENS

It is the new young queen wasps that are mainly responsible for building such nests – or at least, more accurately, for *starting* their construction. First, they look for suitable vegetation, usually pieces of dry wood which they can bite off with their strong jaws and then chew, softening the papery substance into a pulp with the help of their saliva.

Next they form a stalk of paper and make a layer of paper cells, which is suspended from a tree or perhaps inside a building. The cells are of fairly uniform size because the queens use their antennae to measure them. Then they will rest before laying

an egg in each, gluing it firmly in place so that it cannot possibly fall out from the open end of the cell. Usually, there is only a tiny entrance to the nest. This makes it easy to guard from predators, and also helps keep the temperature at an even level.

BIRTH OF A WASP

The eggs soon hatch, and the queen feeds the emerging larvae on bugs that she has killed and brought to the as-yet simple nest, chewing them up to aid the digestion of her offspring. She may even feed them honey.

Whether the females will mature to become fertile queens or sterile workers is very much dependent on their diet. Meanwhile, the only role that a male social wasp will ever have is to mate with future queens. As a rule, he will die shortly afterward.

The emerging larvae that are worker wasps (females) will then take over the job of enlarging the nest, together with care of the next generation. There are many layers of paper, and air becomes trapped between each so that the nest is kept warm. Soon, the paper nest will be home to several thousands of wasps – workers, drones and new queens among them.

FACTFILE

Some species of wasps make homes in other ways – from mud, in holes, or they may even take up residence in the nests of other bugs.

A varied family

There are thousands of species of wasps – some large, some small, some striped and some jewel-colored.

Not all wasps have the black and yellow stripes that are the hallmarks of many familiar species, such as the paper wasp, shown *bottom right*. It looks like the common wasp, except that it has a more pear-shaped thorax and abdomen that make it recognizable.

The tarantula wasp, *right*, meanwhile, with its magnificent amber-coloured wings and curled antennae, is the largest wasp in the entire world, and hunts for spiders, in a method described on page 60.

Other sorts of wasps, such as the emerald-colored one from India, *top right*, also hunt and sting insect prey, such as cockroaches, for the benefit of their future offspring.

The ichneumon wasp, which leads a solitary life, will lay her eggs deep inside the wood of a tree, rather than within a nest. First, though, she has to pick the right tree. She does this by

tapping at it with her antennae. If it seems to be hollow, there could be wood wasp larvae within, and she will have struck lucky. She would like to get at them for the sake of the next generation. Now she will start to drill with her extremely long ovipositor (this organ is longer than the rest of her body!) She lays her eggs *inside* the bodies of the wood wasp larvae, and manages to hit the target even though she cannot

FACTFILE

Sand wasps are unusual in that they make their nests in soil that is sandy, the whole process taking several hours of hard labor.

58

World of the wasp

- Wasps are very important pest-controllers. In the spring and summer, they eat vast numbers of pest insects, such as caterpillars and sawfly larvae.

see into the hole she has bored. When her own larvae hatch, they will be able to feed on the bodies of their hosts, until they are of sufficient size to chew their way out and to emerge from the confines of the tree.

INSIDE A GALL

Did you know that oak apples (or galls) are actually made by insect larvae, and sometimes by the larvae of so-called gall wasps? Occasionally, they make their galls on roses. These wasps lay their eggs on a plant – sometimes even on part of the root – and when the larvae hatch, the plant tissue surrounding them swells. This is to the larvae's advantage, providing them with food and protection from predators. In some instances, several larvae may even develop within the same gall. These galls can vary a lot in shape, size and color – it all depends on the type of gall wasp that laid the egg in the first place, since there are many species.

TINIEST OF ALL

One of the smallest wasps of all is minute and known as the chalcid wasp. Though tiny, they have a very important role, since they are prime controllers of several sorts of pest, including the larvae of the cabbage white butterfly.

Behavior patterns

So varied is the appearance of the whole family of wasps that it is perhaps not surprising that they differ so much in their type of behavior, too.

Common wasps are adept at paper-making for their nests, as described on pages 56-57. But did you know that certain others are more like potters, building their homes from mud or clay? Many of them even add pebbles to the walls of these constructions so that they finally look like miniature stone-built edifices, the mud merely resembling packing material. The gold-faced potter wasp, however, found in Brazil, is an even more creative architect, building in the shape of a water jug, its nest most often to be found not out-of-doors but within a human shelter.

Digger wasps are particularly good at tunneling underground. One of the largest species of wasps and also one of the fiercest, they can drive shafts down into the earth, and will often extend them with branches, ending in small cells. Each chamber, or cell, is for one of the digger's eggs.

First, though, the wasp makes sure that each cell is well-stocked with food for the larvae. To this end, the digger wasp seeks out a cicada and will sting it so that it is paralyzed, even though this insect is twice the wasp's size. It is not a problem for the wasp to find such prey; male cicadas sing so loudly that they positively advertise their presence. The wasp then flies with its victim to the shaft. The developing larvae will not go hungry.

SPIDER-HUNTERS

Some wasps are very particular about their prey — spider wasps, for instance; and even within this group, certain spider wasps will only bother to hunt down certain types of spiders. They then paralyze their prey with their stinger, and bury the unfortunate victim, laying their eggs nearby.

There are even female spider-hunting wasps that get other species to do their killing for them. They wait for another type of spider-hunting wasp to bury its latest victim and then invade to lay their own eggs. The larvae from these develop more rapidly and will devour not only the eggs that were first laid but also the first wasp's prey. What very selfish behavior this is!

World of the wasp

- Wasps help in the fight against certain insect pests because, as larvae, they get their sustenance from such meals.

FACTFILE

Wasps love to feed on ripe fruit, and a few are able to demolish an apple, just like the one shown *right*, in a very short time.

61

Lacewings

Although they have four wings, lacewings are not strong fliers and will not venture far afield, tending to flutter through the air instead, almost as gently as a snowflake.

There are several species of lacewing in addition to the golden brown one, shown landing on a flower in the illustration featured, *right*. The green lacewing, for example, is quite common in the British Isles. It is also known as the golden-eye, a name taken from its prominent, bright but deep yellow-colored organs of sight.

SMELLY BUGS

All lacewings are beautiful, delicate-looking creatures, with attractively marked transparent wings. Yet some species are known for the very unpleasant smell that they exude – which is why they are sometimes given the further alternative name of stink flies, even though they are not true flies. Indeed, as you can see, they more closely resemble dragonflies.

Both the green and the brown lacewings are also

Flying wing

Compound eye

surprisingly cunning and keen predators, in spite of their small size. (Some are no longer than your upper thumb joint.) The larvae are predatory, too. A number are even cannibalistic and will feed on their siblings.

The first larva to emerge from one of a clutch of eggs has even been spotted sitting in wait for others to hatch, and then promptly devouring them, in preference to local greenfly.

World of the lacewing

- Lacewings are often at risk of being hunted by bats at night but may detect their squeaking and so be able to take prompt evasive action.

STICKY STUFF

The larvae hatch from eggs that are laid on stalk-like structures so that they resemble a plant of some kind. When she is ready to lay, the female lacewing will secrete a tiny globule of sticky liquid and this adheres the egg-structure to the leaf or shoot on which it is to be deposited. These eggs have been described as looking like the fruit of a type of moss.

The larvae are certainly greedy, and have sharp jaws that resemble a pair of calipers. What is more, they have a most curious habit concerning the bugs, such as aphids, on which they like to feed. They suck them dry but, then, instead of discarding the husks, they place them on their backs. Here, the husks dry and become shriveled. Each time they molt, the larvae lose this layer of husks. But with their very next meal, they start to build up a husk-covered back once more. This is an odd mode of behavior; but when they are covered with many such husks, the larvae are, of course, very well camouflaged from predators. It certainly makes them very hard to spot on plants, even when you know that they are there.

Abdomen

Hind wings

FACTFILE

No wonder lacewings are loved by gardeners: their grubs feed on greenfly and other pests which will so often destroy plants.

63

Doodlebugs

The largest of these remarkable insects are just 3in (8cm) long; yet they have proved to be the wiliest of predators.

Doodlebugs may look a little like dragonflies or lacewings at first glance; but, in fact, it is not that difficult to spot the difference if you look closely – because their antennae are thickly clubbed at the ends, unlike those of dragonflies or lacewings, which are fine.

Doodlebugs certainly have a curious-sounding name – the same name, in fact, as a World War II flying bomb, although this weapon was nicknamed entirely independently and has no association with the insect.

MASTERS OF AMBUSH
The doodlebug has the alternative name of ant lion, and this is closely related to the behavior of the larvae of many species of doodlebugs. These normally live in sandy soil and dig out little pits for themselves.

World of the doodlebug

- Most of the six hundred species of these insects are found in tropical regions, but some doodlebugs are native to Europe and the USA.

They then bury themselves at the bottom, exposing only their jaws. Small creatures, such as ants, may then fall into the pit and be seized by the camouflaged ant lion or doodlebug, just as you can see at the bottom of the illustration *opposite*.

LONG LIFE CYCLE
It can take as long as two years or more for a doodlebug to develop from the egg into its mature adult form. The larvae molt a few times while growing, and then pupate under the sand inside a silk cocoon.

Surprisingly, the silk is produced through the doodlebug's anus. The caterpillars of butterflies and moths, on the other hand, produce silk through special glands in their heads.

After pupation, it will take only about a month for the winged doodlebug to emerge. The pupa gets out of its cocoon by cutting a hole in it. For this, its strong jaws come in very useful. All this takes place underground, so that the mature doodlebug must now get to the surface and hang from a plant while its body and its wings harden.

SHADY SPOTS
Look out for doodlebugs wherever there is fine, sandy soil in woodlands or under overhanging rocks, where the larvae will be well-sheltered from inclement weather.

Cicadas

Mainly found in tropical regions of the world, cicadas are best known for their delightful songs.

If it seems to be raining slightly, yet the sky is completely clear, it could be that cicadas are feeding up in a tree and excreting sugary water that feels and looks like drizzle.

You would be lucky to spot a cicada. They are generally well camouflaged. It may even be one of the North American species that spends as long as 17 years underground as a larva before taking on its adult form.

MATING CALL

Undoubtedly one of the most musical of all the insect family, cicadas produce their songs in an entirely different way from those other highly musical insects, the crickets and grasshoppers. Both male and female cicadas are vocal, but it is the males that sing loudest of all. They do this in order to call others of their species together so that mating may proceed with speed and efficiency.

At the bottom of their abdomens, they have two membranes, known as tymbals. These can be pulled and released by a special muscle, and will oscillate rapidly, producing sound. The tune is then greatly amplified and distorted by a chamber that opens and closes around the whole sound-box mechanism.

Some cicadas produce their songs by day; others by night, if they are most active then. They are large for insects, and have broad, sturdy bodies, as you can see from this illustration, flanked by two pairs of transparent veined wings, although the tips of a few species are brightly colored.

DEADLY ENEMIES

One of the largest wasp species found in the United States is the digger wasp. The female is a good parent and will dig a shaft into the ground, building round cells in side branches, ready for egg-laying. But first, it will go hunting for its prey – a large type of cicada that is much bigger than itself and known as

World of the cicada

- Each of the 1,500 or so types of cicadas produces its own tune. An expert can instantly recognize these and will identify the particular species.

- In some parts of Africa, where food is often short, people have been known to eat cicadas, which they cook – but we do not recommend them.

the lyreman (because of the wonderful song it produces).

It is not difficult for the wasp to find a lyreman because of the way in which it proclaims its presence. The wasp then stings it and hauls it to a suitable spot, from where it can take to the air, clutching tightly at its prey. Entomologists have even discovered that one cicada is sufficient to nourish a developing male digger wasp, but that two are required for a developing female. It is a sad ending for such musical bugs!

Listen for the songs of the cicada if you ever travel to tropical regions. Their lovely melody is entrancing.

Locusts

The approach of a swarm of locusts can be terrifying. One, in Morocco, North Africa, in 1955, extended to 155 miles (250km) in length and was 12 miles (20km) wide.

No one needs to fear an ordinary grasshopper. After all, it will not attack or bite you. Instead, it spends most of its time simply eating, basking in the sun, and singing.

But certain large grasshoppers are rather different. They will swarm in enormous numbers and can cause terrible devastation to crops. These dreaded insects are the locusts.

Usually, locusts live on their own. But, if conditions are right and there is plenty of food, they start to breed rapidly. Millions of nymphs will gather in huge groups and march off together, eating any plants in their path. Once they have their wings, they then fly off in huge swarms.

These very frightening insects are generally found only in warm regions of the world. They have enormous appetites and will eat any sort of vegetation available, including cultivated crops. Famine may result.

Many regions of Africa, America, Australia, and Asia have suffered from devastation by locusts; and the cost in money, and in human lives due to starvation, when all available crops are destroyed, can be enormous. Experts estimate that a single locust can eat its own weight in food every day!

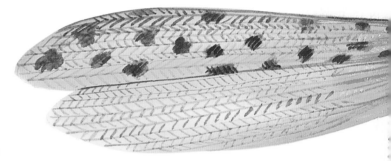

Locusts normally appear after heavy rain when plants start to grow and will provide food for them. Locusts have even been known to travel as far as 3,500 miles (5,600km) over an ocean – quite a journey!

They were also the subject of one of the ten plagues of Egypt, as described in the *Old Testament*, where an east wind brought a horde of locusts which covered the ground until it was black. They devoured everything, even the trees, so nothing green remained in all the land. It is certainly extraordinary that these extremely ravenous mini-beasts are so closely related to the far more peaceful grasshoppers of the countryside.

World of the locust

- A single, enormous swarm of locusts will probably have more of these creatures in it that the whole current human population of our planet.

Bees

If you hear a buzzing sound on a warm summer day, chances are that a bee is hovering over a flower and searching for a giant drink of its nectar! You'll know it immediately, too, by its furry, striped body.

There are over 20,000 different known types of bees and they live in most parts of the world. Those we usually see in gardens or woodlands, however, are bumblebees and honeybees.

Both of these types may look as if their bodies are soft to the touch but, underneath their furry outer covering, is a hard shell of bone. This covers the bee's entire body, which consists of three main parts.

First, there is the head. This has a tongue or proboscis, used for reaching deep inside flowers in order to suck out nectar. Also on its head, a bee has three small eyes at the front, and two larger eyes, one on each side. The two large eyes have over 6,000 lenses each, so the bee can see all around, not just in front. This is extremely useful; a bee often has to spot food from a distance, and it can also check that there are no predators around to chase it.

FACTFILE

Bees are not poisoned by their own stings because only at the moment they sting are the secretions that form the poison mixed.

Pollen basket

It is pitch black inside its nest, so the bee finds its way around by using the two thin antennae situated at the front of its head. A bee can also pass silent messages to other bees by tangling its antennae together with theirs.

Wing

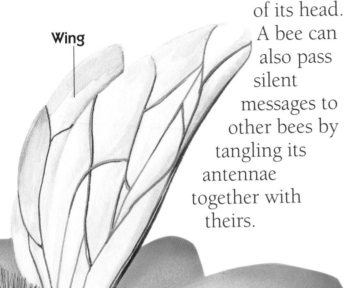

Antenna

World of the bee

- Bees have a double set of wings – two main ones (forewings) and two smaller ones (hindwings). The vibrating wings cause a bee's buzz.

The second part of the bee's body is the thorax, or chest cavity, which supports its six legs. The back legs differ from the front two pairs in that they have wide, flat parts that are fringed with long hairs. These are known as baskets and are especially designed for carrying pollen.

STING IN THE TAIL

The third and largest part of a bee's body is the abdomen. In female bees, this contains the bee's wax-making glands and also its only means of protection – the stinger! Poison is kept at the ready in a long tube just under its tail-end. So beware, and be sure to keep still if a bee is buzzing around you! If you ignore it, chances are that it will ignore you, too, and soon fly off peacefully to find nectar for the hive.

The pollinators

Without insects such as bees, much of the world's vegetation – flowering plants and trees – would suffer to a marked degree.

The bee is a flower's best friend. You may think this odd. After all, the bee drinks its nectar and takes away most of its pollen. But it is all part of a clever plan, and the survival of flowers depends on it.

Like most living things, flowers have to produce new ones to replace them when they die. For this to happen, the pollen has to mix with tiny eggs to make seeds. This process is known as pollination.

But a flower cannot do this by itself – it has no moving parts! So what better form of transportation for the pollen than a furry bee looking for a drink!

As a bee climbs right into the flower for its nectar, the long hairs on its coat brush up against pollen. It is usually a tight squeeze inside a flower so, on the way out, a lot of the pollen is brushed off the bee. The pollen now falls on to the parts of the flower that need to be pollinated to form seeds.

The bee is a lifesaver for trees, too. Pollen from male apple trees, for instance, has to find its way to the female trees. In the spring, these trees produce sweet-smelling blossoms that attract the bees so that they flit from tree to tree, seeking out all the glorious nectar available.

Pollen from one tree sticks to the bee's furry body, and some of the pollen drops off when it lands on the next apple tree. So without the flower's best friend, there would be no more apple trees, either!

FACTFILE

Only female bees will sting because the stinging apparatus is an organ called an ovipositor, once used for egg-laying.

World of the bee

- Colonies of honey bees last for several years, although new queens may sometimes replace old ones during this time.

A hive of activity

Inside any hive, there is always a tremendous amount of activity taking place as the workers accomplish their vital tasks.

What is life like for worker honey bees? They are very important; in fact, the colony could not do without them. There would be no hive and, if they did not do their job, no honey to enjoy. But although they are all female, they cannot lay eggs, as the queen bee can.

Even when still very young, these workers are kept endlessly busy. They will help clean out the nest and also collect nectar from older bees, feeding it to the hungry baby bees, as in the illustration, *right*. Once these are a little older, the workers are sent to guard the entrance to the nest.

FACTFILE

Before sugar cane and sugar beets, the honey provided by bees was the only way of sweetening our food.

TIRELESS COLLECTORS

In one colony alone, there may be as many as 60,000 workers! These eventually become foragers, whose job it is to find flowers and collect nectar and pollen from them. When they have as much as they can carry, they return home to unload it all, repeating the task a great many times throughout the day until it gets dark.

Worker bee

Cell cap

At nightfall, these hard-working females can rest. But they will have to be up again with the sun, ready to go out for the next day's food. A nest or hive needs large numbers of these females to keep it going.

DANCE ROUTINES

The workers find their way backward and forward to the nest by the angle of the sun. They can also let each other know where there is nectar by

doing a special dance. If they do a round dance, the nectar is nearby. If they wag their abdomens, however, this means that the nectar is far away.

The noise that bees make, meanwhile, indicates the quantity and the quality of the source of nectar. If they make a great deal of noise, this is a sign that the source is plentiful. The dancing bees also supply samples of the nectar to help the workers identify it.

EVICTED MALES

Male honey bees, which are bigger but fewer in number, are known as drones and do not work at all. Their task is to mate with the queen bee so she can lay eggs. The males generally die directly after they have mated.

But even the worker bees have a short life – honey bee workers, for instance, only live for about six or seven weeks on average. Worker bees never seem to waste a minute, though! No wonder we use the phrase "as busy as a bee!"

A queen's speech

What would a queen honey bee have to tell you about life in a hive, if only she could speak? Read on and find out.

I'm the honey bee queen, and I'm in charge of the hive. You can see me in the center of this picture. Without me, there wouldn't be any other bees at all. That's because only *I* can lay eggs; so the others fuss around me all day, licking and grooming me, and making sure I always have plenty to eat.

I'm nearly twice the size of the other bees in the hive. This is because when I was a baby, I was fed mountains of rich food, called royal jelly, which my workers themselves produce in their bodies.

A queen like me can live for four or five years, much longer than other bees. I rarely leave the hive, though, except for mating, when I fly out to attract a drone by my scent. We mate in flight, and then I return. Laying thousands of eggs takes up most of my time. Each has to be laid in a place of its own, where it can hatch in safety.

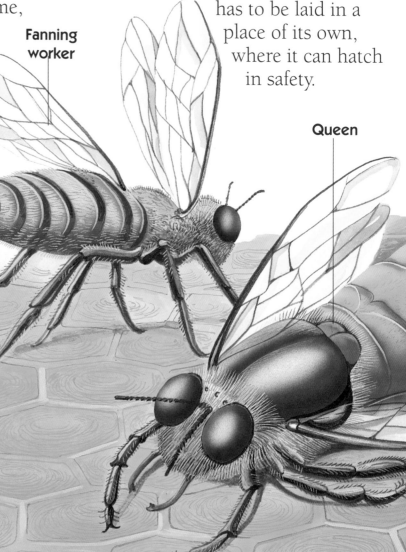

Fanning worker

Queen

Cell with pupa

FACTFILE

A queen mates only once in her lifetime, and the drone that succeeds in mating with her dies soon after.

My worker bees build thousands of six-sided chambers, or cells, made of wax, and these form the comb. I back into each cell in turn and lay one egg, about the size of a pinhead, in each. A sticky substance that I exude ensures they stay put in the cells. Some of the eggs are fertilized and will produce females. Unfertilized eggs, meanwhile, produce males.

World of the bee

- The queen secretes a special food called the queen substance, which the workers all share, passing it on from one to another.

- Only the drones and the queen are fertile. No other bees can ever reproduce in any way.

After three days, they hatch into grubs, or larvae. Worker bees feed them on royal jelly to help them grow. But they only get a little royal jelly so that the female bees will not grow up into queens. Only one queen rules the hive, and that's *me*!

In just a few days, the larvae have grown so big that they fill the cells, which are closed with a wax seal by my loyal workers. The larvae now gradually change into pupae, which look like white bees without wings. Twelve days pass before they are mature enough to chew their way out of their waxy cots.

Soon, my hive will be full-to-bursting with bees. When there's hardly room to breathe, it's time for some of us to go. Lots of my workers gather round me and we leave together to start a new colony.

Time to swarm

Sometimes, the population of a hive becomes too great. When this happens, it is time for some of the inhabitants to leave in a swarm.

Now imagine *you* are a queen honey bee. You have been so good at laying eggs that there is now hardly any room to move inside your hive.

You know, however, that you cannot go before a new replacement queen has been raised. She has to be hatched within an especially large cell since, like you, the future queen is going to grow quickly and to a large size.

When you are ready to leave, you will take some worker bees with you to forage for food. A few drones will come along, too; but the other drones will stay behind and will mate with the newly-raised queen.

Swarming usually happens on a bright, sunny day, and at around noon, as in this illustration. Back at the hive, meanwhile, the new queen will have

emerged and will be stinging to death all her rivals as they, too, are born.

All the travelers leave the hive together, and your swarm makes a dazzling sight. Hundreds of you all squeeze tightly together in a buzzing mass as you fly to a nearby tree and rest.

But where do you all go? Before you left the hive, a few scout bees had gone out house-hunting on your behalf. Once they found what seemed a safe place for a home, they communicated its whereabouts to all the bees in the swarm by performing a special dance, just as they do when advising about a food store.

Whether it is a hollow tree they have found, or a nest left by a bird or mouse, you will soon be settled, and your workers will build new cells in which more eggs can be laid.

FACTFILE

One of the main enemies of bees is the Death's Head Hawk-moth. It will frequently try to enter hives and steal the honey.

Making honey

Don't you just love honey on bread or warm muffins? Jam, of course, is made by humans from fruit. But honey is made by the honeybee.

Hives are usually built where there is easy access to plenty of flowers and trees. Someone who keeps bees is called an apiarist, while the wooden hive built specially by apiarists as a home for honey bees is called an apiary.

others of their find. The information is passed on by means of a dance, containing secret clues. If the forager bees run around in small circles, this means that the flowers are less than 80ft (25m) away. They will have struck lucky! But if they perform a figure-eight dance, then the source is farther away, perhaps even as far as 330ft (100m).

These words come from the Latin or scientific name for a honey bee, which is *Apis*.

At first, a few adventurous forager bees will leave the hive in search of sweet nectar, and also pollen. Then, once they have located an ideal food source, they return to the hive to tell the

When the workers get to the food source, they will crawl right inside the flowers and lick the nectar with their long proboscis. They store the nectar in a special stomach known as a crop or honey-stomach; and once this is full, they will make their way back.

The hive bees now set to work on the nectar. The workers breathe on it first to evaporate the water. Then, once the runny nectar gets thick and sticky, they carry it to specially-built cells.

After a few days, proud beekeepers simply lift out the honeycombs and scrape off the honey, using a machine called an extractor. Of course, they have to

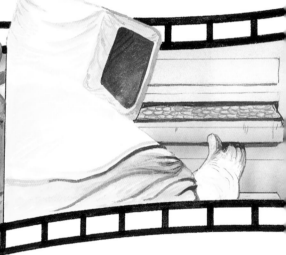

FACTFILE

The Romans were very keen bee-keepers and loved to eat honey. They built hives for their bees in all sorts of different shapes.

wear protective veils or helmets as well as special suits, or they would be liable to be stung repeatedly. Bees are no great respecters of their keepers! Soon the honey can be packed into jars, and will be ready for our supermarket shelves.

As well as honey, bees also make wax which we use to make candles or polish. They produce a substance called propolis, too. This is a resin used to strengthen their combs and thought to have health-giving properties for humans.

World of the bee

- Hives have to be well-ventilated. The beekeeper usually sees to this. But if by chance a hive gets too hot, bees do this themselves, fanning the air furiously with their wings.

Grasshoppers

City-dwellers rarely see them. But most people who live in the country are familiar with grasshoppers, and certainly *hear* them.

Katydids like grass, but will also eat small insects and centipedes, and may even turn cannibalistic if they do not find enough food to eat or enough space to live in.

Both sorts of grasshopper have two antennae on their heads. Those on the true grasshoppers (short-horns), as their

Grasshoppers belong to a family of insects known as the *Orthoptera*. Within this group, they are divided into long-horns and short-horns. The 'horns' in these names are the antennae on top of these insects' heads.

Long-horns, like the one *far right*, are also known as bush-crickets or katydids; while short-horns, like the one *above*, are true grasshoppers.

Both types have very solid heads with two compound eyes, one on either side. Most also have quite powerful jaws for cutting through their food.

World of the grasshopper

- Some grasshoppers have fascinating names – the Great Shielded grasshopper of New Guinea, for instance.

In addition to their role as coverings for the wings that the grasshopper uses to fly, the outer pair of wings also carries special sound equipment for production of the grasshopper's song. However, although it may seem strange, some types of grasshopper do not have wings at all or are endowed with just poorly-developed ones.

Grasshoppers can vary in size. The European long-nosed species, for example, is 2.5in (6.35cm) long. But one South American grasshopper measures all of 6in (15cm).

name suggests, are shorter and thicker than those of the katydids. These are delicate sense organs that are used for feeling, and look a bit like radio aerials.

Grasshoppers have three pairs of legs. The first two are for walking, while the third larger pair have strong muscles for jumping. Sometimes the back legs are even a different color.

INFREQUENT FLYERS

Most types of grasshoppers have two pairs of wings, but only one of these pairs is used for flying. The other pair just provides a protective layer for when the grasshopper is simply resting or hopping.

Camouflage by color

It is often difficult to spot grasshoppers because their coloring tends to provide excellent camouflage. If you do find one, however, you can tell if it is a female because of the egg-placer appendage at the end of its body.

Many grasshoppers have suitable coloring for their environment so that they can hide themselves within their habitat and stay safe from predators.

Those that live in the desert or in muddy areas, for example, tend not to be green in color, while those that live in the tropics tend to be the same color

as grass. Such coloring provides excellent camouflage for them.

Some grasshoppers are even cave dwellers. These have no wings but very long legs and lengthy antennae.

It is not always possible, even for an entomologist, however, to identify a specific type of grasshopper simply by its color. This is because even grasshoppers of the same type may sometimes have a different shade of the same color, or varying body patterns featuring spots or stripes.

MASTER OF DISGUISE

Amazingly, one African bush-cricket, or katydid, found in the Sudan, can go so far as to disguise itself as an ant. This is a useful trick in areas where whole armies of ants are known to attack grasshoppers.

World of the grasshopper

- There are thousands of different grasshopper species, among them the well-known green, field, meadow and mottled grasshoppers.

A grasshopper may also look like a blade of grass, a leaf, or a twig, and its enemies will not be able to recognize it.

GIANT LEAPS

But if, by chance, it is disturbed, a grasshopper can spring rapidly into action by using its powerful back legs to leap away from danger. You can see one doing this in the illustration featured here. The others that are nearby would probably soon follow suit.

FACTFILE

True grasshoppers are completely vegetarian, and the main items on their menu are grass, leaves, flowers, and bits of fruit.

Emerging nymphs

If you see a grasshopper jumping, it may be escaping from a predator, or it could be a display flight, which is performed prior to mating.

Soon after mating, a female grasshopper lays a batch of 30-100 eggs, releasing them into the ground in a special covering called an egg-pod. She may even lay up to ten batches of eggs at a time.

Just figure it out! This makes it possible for her to produce up to one thousand babies.

The female grasshopper will bury her pods by pushing them down into the soft earth with her abdomen. To make sure the pods are buried deeply enough, she inflates her abdomen, making it four times the size it would be normally. This means that she can dig very deep holes for her egg-pods. Then, after 2-4 weeks, the eggs hatch.

World of the grasshopper

- Although usually well-camouflaged, some grasshoppers have flashes of bright coloring on their wings, which they use to startle a predator.

- Some grasshoppers are very fussy about the plants they will feed on. Others, however, enjoy a wide variety of vegetation.

The tiny creatures emerging are known as nymphs. At this stage, they are rather odd-looking, as you can see in the sequence *below*.

But they will soon start to shed their skin in a process known as molting. In all, the young grasshoppers will molt between five and eight more times, gradually increasing in size. At the same time, their wings will also be developing, ready for flight.

Soon they will make their first flight away from their hatching ground; and within a few weeks, these young grasshoppers will be ready to take their own turn at producing a new generation.

As yet, however, they are not at all like the brightly colored and very tuneful insects that they will soon become on reaching maturity.

Then, at last, the day comes for the nymphs to shed their skin for the final time. They will now hang on a twig or some other convenient resting place and let their wings dry. What beautiful creatures they have become!

FACTFILE

Grasshoppers have a spring mechanism in their knees and strong leg muscles that enable them to jump considerable distances.

Love songs

The song of a grasshopper can usually best be heard in the evening when all is quiet.

If you have ever walked through a field filled with a curious chirping sound, chances are that it was being made not by a bird but by male grasshoppers.

To make their song, most male grasshoppers rub part of their legs against the thickest veins on their outer wings, in much the same way that a violinist will move the bow over the strings of his violin. This process is called "stridulation."

Each type of grasshopper makes a slightly different sound. Many experts can even identify a specific type of grasshopper just by listening to the sound it makes. The faster a male grasshopper rubs its legs against its wings, the higher the sound will be. So grasshoppers making slow strokes will produce just a low hum.

Male grasshoppers sing for several reasons, but perhaps the most important is to catch the attention of a female. Scientists have even played back recordings of a male grasshopper's song to a female, which will all at once start to get very excited.

FACTFILE

Katydids (the long-horned grasshoppers) usually live at a higher level than the so-called true or short-horned grasshoppers.

The females of one particular type of grasshopper also sing. However, they do this not to attract a mate, but possibly to scare off enemies.

HEARING LEGS

Male bush-crickets, or katydids (the long-horn grasshoppers), make their songs in another way, not with their legs but by rubbing the tops of their wings together. These insects have their ears hidden away in tiny slits in their legs. If you ever get the chance to observe a bush cricket close-up, you may notice that it sometimes swings its legs back and forth. If it does so, you can be almost certain that it is a female listening out for a male's song.

There are other types of grasshopper, meanwhile, that have their hearing organs on the last part of the thorax, or even on their abdomens.

If you would like to keep a grasshopper for a while to observe it, you might try to catch one, very gently, using a butterfly net. Then, keep it in a tank with a net covering so that it can breathe. Feed it fresh grass and leaves, but be sure to return it to the wild after a couple of days, since grasshoppers prefer the great outdoors.

World of the grasshopper

- Some grasshoppers will produce a foul-smelling fluid if a predator approaches, in order to warn its enemy that it will not make a tasty meal.

On the ground

Outdoors, many thousands of bugs live most of their lives down at ground level, although some will also take to the air at times.

Ground-dwelling bugs are all around us, wherever we live. Some are in the soil, and you will come across them when you are gardening – worms, slugs, snails, ants, and centipedes, for instance. But do you know anything about their secret lives – how they mate, what they eat, and the way in which they try to deal with predators? Lots of other bugs, meanwhile, could be hiding in the vegetation, well camouflaged from enemies. There may be pests, too, at ground level – weevils, perhaps.

And have you ever considered that there could be many bugs in your home? We are all familiar with the house spider. But why do we so often find them in the bathtub? Why do we need to check our pet dogs or cats for fleas? And what should you do if you ever spot cockroaches in your kitchen, hunting for scraps that will provide a good meal for them? It's an equally unpleasant thought but lice can infest your hair. This is not a disgrace, though, because anyone can catch them through close contact.

Of course, if you travel to tropical regions, you may come across more exotic creepy-crawlies – termites, maybe, or the fearsome scorpion with its deadly sting. Be prepared for all kinds of ground-dwelling bugs, as presented in the following section.

Scorpions

What a fierce-looking creature a scorpion is! In fact, it is almost as if its very appearance provides a warning to keep away.

It will not be easy for you to spot a scorpion in the wild because they are mostly out and about at night. Even then, they will almost certainly be aware of your approach. Once they sense your presence, they will normally scuttle away to hide in the nearest hole to conceal themselves – beneath a piece of tree bark, for instance, or maybe under some dead leaves.

Scorpions have a worldwide reputation for being quite scary-looking. And, by nature, they often live up to their appearance, because some of them can kill you with their sting. They have even been known to be hostile to one another on occasions.

As you can see in the illustration shown here,

their bodies are divided into segments, and they have a pair of large claws that seem out of proportion with their bodies. As a rule, the largest scorpions are usually darkest in color, and smaller ones are paler.

The whole body of a scorpion is covered with a tough coating. In many ways, this is like a soldier's armor. At the front of the mouth, there is one pair of small pincers (known as pedipalps), which the scorpion uses for holding food while it eats.

The scorpion's thorax has four parts to it, each with a pair of legs. Then comes the abdomen, at the end of which is the stinger for which it is so famous.

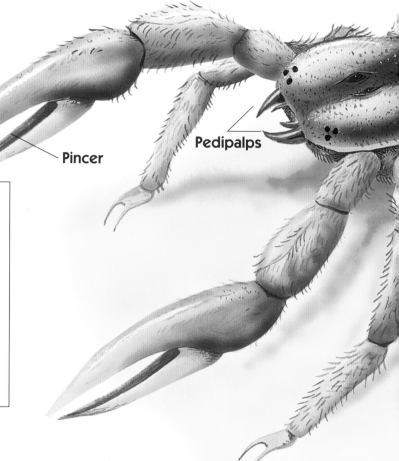

Pincer

Pedipalps

World of the scorpion

- Scorpions have a substance in their bodies that glows in ultraviolet light. So if scientists are searching for them, they use an ultraviolet lamp, which shows the creatures up beautifully.

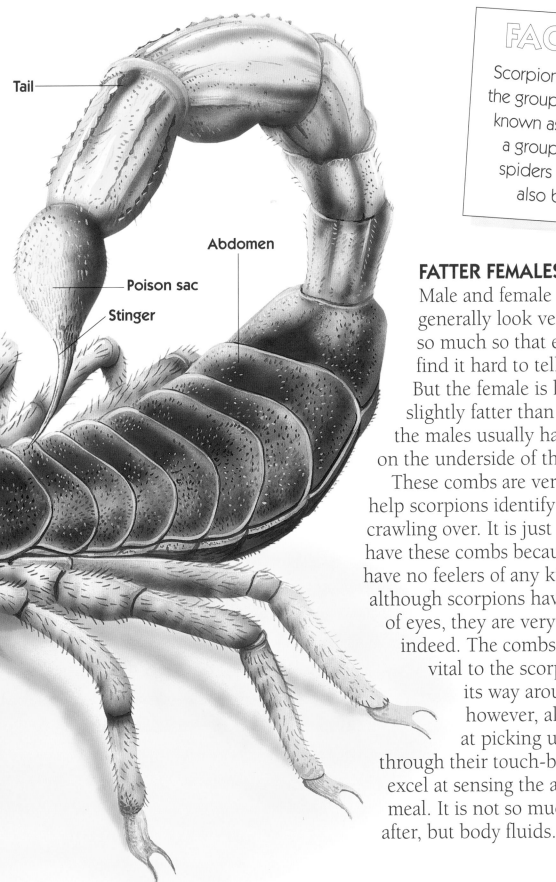

Tail

Abdomen

Poison sac

Stinger

FATTER FEMALES

Male and female scorpions generally look very much alike, so much so that even experts find it hard to tell them apart. But the female is likely to be slightly fatter than the male, and the males usually have larger combs on the underside of the abdomen. These combs are very sensitive and help scorpions identify what they are crawling over. It is just as well that they have these combs because scorpions have no feelers of any kind. And although scorpions have several pairs of eyes, they are very short-sighted indeed. The combs, therefore, are vital to the scorpion for finding its way around. They are, however, also highly skilled at picking up vibrations through their touch-bristles, and they excel at sensing the approach of a meal. It is not so much flesh they are after, but body fluids.

93

Desert-dwellers

Be sure to watch out for the deadly scorpion, if traveling in one of the world's tropical regions!

From time to time, scorpions turn up in the oddest places – England, for example, where most types are not found naturally. It is probably because they managed to creep into someone's luggage or into a crate of imported tropical fruit. Most scorpions like warmth. They usually prefer, therefore, to live in a desert environment, such as the African Sahara, in parts of Arizona in the United States, or in the Australian outback.

They also like to live in the dense undergrowth of rain forests, such as those in South America. To avoid the excessive heat of the day in such regions, they will sometimes try to burrow into the ground or perhaps hide under any available stones. But scorpions also have another way of cooling down when the weather gets too hot for comfort.

KEEPING COOL

Scorpions are able to straighten their legs and stand so that their bodies are elevated and do not touch the ground, as you can see in the illustration shown here. This stance allows more air to circulate around them and goes a long way toward lowering their body temperature.

Scorpions can go without having a drink of water for months at a time. This is important since so many of them live in hot places, where water is often scarce. They get most of the liquid their bodies need from the insects and other creatures that they eat. But they do like to drink water from time to time, and will also lap up morning dew.

World of the scorpion

- Scorpions are often attracted by the glow of a campfire, the same way that moths are to an electric light or candle.

Getting together

In all, there are about 650 different types of scorpions, ranging in size from 0.2in (0.5cm) to an awesome 8in (20cm) long.

Scorpions are usually lone creatures, living a solitary life rather than in colonies. So, in many ways, both sexes are rather fortunate if they manage to come across a mate at all.

When they do, it is not always instant attraction, however. First, a complicated courtship ritual has to take place. The male will face the female and then grasp her claws with his claws. At this point, it looks very much as if they are having fun and dancing together!

LOVE GAMES

If the female resists his advances, however, the male may threaten her with his stinger. She is just as clever, though, and may threaten him back with hers. Once he has won her over, which he usually does, the male then drags the female to a suitable area for the mating ritual.

He now proceeds to scrape at the soil with his feet and makes a hollow. Here, he deposits his sperm, which the female will take up. Now comes the real drama because, sometimes, the female will

actually devour the male after mating. This is not the kindest way for the female to treat the father of her babies! But she does get a highly nutritious meal which will help her produce strong offspring.

FACTFILE

Whip-scorpions, which are related to true scorpions, do not sting, secreting an irritating substance instead to deter an attacker.

Male

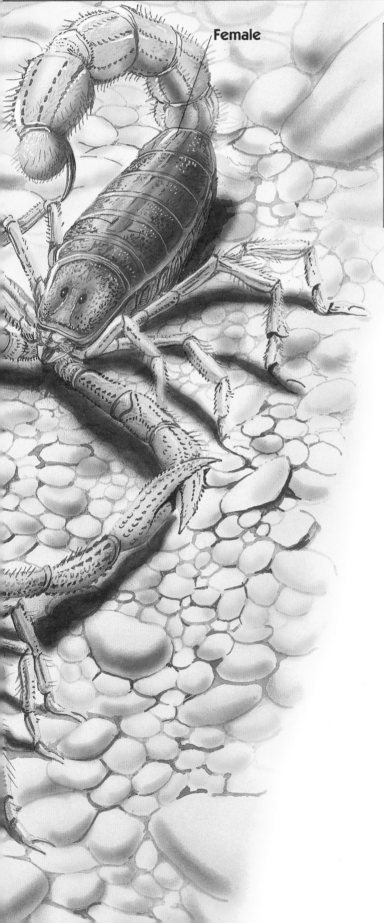

Female

World of the scorpion

- If an enemy, such as the camel spider – a savage carnivore – manages to sever a scorpion's stinger, it will be the victor in the battle for survival.

Young scorpions do not hatch from eggs but are born alive to the female a few weeks later.

EASY-RIDERS

When the babies are born, they are less than one-eighth the size of their mothers but look just like them. They emerge inside a skin covering, which their mothers have to open with their stingers to release them. They will now climb on to their mothers' back until they are able to look after themselves. Sometimes, one female may have so many young ones on her back that she has a furry appearance.

The young are colorless at first and not very strong, so they sometimes slip off their mothers' back. But they soon grow and will molt about seven times before they reach full adult size.

False scorpions – distantly related to true scorpions but without a stinger – are only 0.5in (1.25cm) long. They, too, hitch lifts from passing insects, but by grabbing onto their legs.

Sting in the tail

Emergency! If a scorpion stings, the unfortunate victim must receive medical attention immediately. His or her life could be in danger.

Somewhere in Africa, a young boy has collapsed. Lying there, the sweat pouring from his face and body, he suddenly finds it difficult to breathe and begins to vomit. His limbs have also gone numb. Then, suddenly, he starts to froth alarmingly at the mouth.

There is no time to lose! He must be rushed to a hospital while there is still a chance that doctors may be able to treat him and save his life. He has been stung by one of the most venomous scorpions of all, and feels terribly sick.

Unfortunately, humans do not have good enough hearing to recognize the peculiar sound made by this desert creature as a warning. The scorpion had been rubbing part of its body against a leg to produce an odd purring noise, but the boy was unaware of this.

Not all scorpions will sting to the death in this way. In fact, most are only

FACTFILE

Legend has it that scorpions carry an oil in their bodies that will cure their own stings, but no one has yet proved this.

98

World of the scorpion

- Once, two hundred scorpions were left alone in a cage for a while. Eventually, there remained only one severely overweight scorpion, surrounded by the remains of the others. They can survive without much food for months but, if starved, larger ones sometimes turn cannibalistic.

dangerous if annoyed or provoked. Lots of scorpion stings are just like wasp stings. But some can be fatal. So they are always to be avoided, just in case.

PAINFUL ATTACK

Disturb a scorpion and it will hold out its pincers, curving its tail right over its back, ready to stab at you with its stinger.

It is the tip of the scorpion's stinger that injects the venom, and this is supplied by two large glands.

Being stung by a scorpion is not as unlikely as one might suppose. It may seem hard to believe but, in some warm countries, and also in the United States, statistics show that more people are killed by scorpions each year than as a result of venomous snake bites.

The sting of the scorpion is, in fact, so painful that the name *scorpion* was given to a medieval form of whip with steel spikes, used as a terrible form of punishment.

Snails

If you spot a slimy trail winding in loops all over a path, a snail has doubtless been out and about. The mucus that a snail makes is sticky and helps it to climb up walls without falling, too.

It is easy to recognize a snail because it always has a shell. If it does not have a shell at all, but looks just like the inside of a snail, it is probably a slug. You can find out all about slugs if you turn to pages 108-109.

Snail shells come in all sorts of shapes and sizes. They can be round or pointed, smooth or knobbly. Many are a drab brown color, with a few spots and marks. Others may have bright red and yellow lines.

But what is a snail like inside its shell? It has no face like yours. Instead, at the front end, there are four spikes, two of

Growth lines

World of the snail

- All the snails on a farm that breed Giant African land snails once escaped and soon began to devastate all the crops in the fields nearby.

which are small and two, large. At the end of each of the large spikes is a tiny eye. A snail cannot see much, but it can recognize if it is light or dark. The two small spikes or tentacles can also smell, taste and feel, helping the snail to know where its next meal is coming from.

Behind the small tentacles lies the snail's mouth. A snail has a tongue that is very different from yours. Called a radula, it has up to 25,000 "teeth" or sharp edges. The snail patiently grinds its way through food using these. You can even *hear* it munching through crisp lettuce!

Where the snail's body meets its shell there is a frill of flesh, known as the mantle, which protects the snail's body inside the shell. And the hole in a snail's right side leads into a space called the mantle cavity, which helps it to breathe.

A snail's shell has growth lines, just like a tree, so you can tell how old a snail is by the number of lines it has there. It is made of strong, chalky material that helps keep out heat, cold, and unwanted strangers – in fact, just like *your* home does.

Shell

FACTFILE

Garden snails are small, only about 2in (5cm) long; but the Giant African land snail normally grows to 8in (20cm) in length.

Eye

Eye stalk

Tentacle

Taking shelter

Lovers of damp weather and uncomfortable in heat, snails need to find shade when it gets hot.

Imagine you are a snail and have been up all night, munching your way through an old cabbage leaf. The sun begins to peep over the horizon. Oh no, not another hot day!

Like all snails, you like it best when the weather is damp, but not raining. You do not really like getting yourself wet. But dry, sunny summer days will be the death of you if you do not get indoors quickly.

If you have been clever, you will have slithered to a shady spot, like the inside of a plant pot, as shown here, or the side of a leafy tree.

If not, you will just have to clamp the open end of your shell down hard on the hot ground and then hope for the best.

One or two of your cousins have a front door, called an operculum, to slam shut against such searing heat.

> ## FACTFILE
> Snails do not have a brain like yours but a system of nerves, helping to warn them of any danger that may be present.

Others quickly produce a sticky mucus plug, or epiphragm, and cram it over the hole in their shells.

You do this in the winter, too, because you do not like the cold, either. Besides, in winter there is hardly anything to eat, and you need to find a safe space where you can rest.

Under a stone or a fallen branch is an ideal spot, as is a crack in a wall.

It is important to stay out of sight. You remain still for weeks at a time during the winter, but hungry birds will be around. They could be desperate for a good meal, and might well enjoy snails for dinner.

You will know when it is time to start moving and feeding after the winter hibernation. The weather will feel warmer, and you can now stretch yourself out. Then you can look for your first great feast of the year — a few fresh lettuce leaves, perhaps!

103

Hermaphrodites

Known for their lack of speed when moving, snails are also slow when getting together to mate.

Most types of living things are divided into males and females. But snails are not. Instead, they are both male and female rolled into one body. This type of creature is known as a hermaphrodite.

But snails still like to cuddle up to each other as part of the mating process, just like lots of other creatures, in spite of being hermaphrodites. So when one snail wants to mate with another snail, it will glide up to a likely partner. It does this at its usual slow pace. Then, they both begin to perform a kind of dance.

other better by stroking each other's tentacles.

Eventually, the snails lie with their right sides together. This is the closest that they can get to one another because of the bulky shells that they carry on their backs.

The male and female parts of the snail's body are situated just behind its head. So when two snails lie closely together side by side, they each are capable of playing the part of both the female and male, like the true hermaphrodites that they are.

Really, they are just circling around to see if they like the look of each other. They will now try to get to know each

World of the snail

- If the outer casing of a snail gets broken, it cannot repair itself and the snail will die.

Snails do nothing fast and even mating can take several hours. But, as if to keep themselves from dozing off or losing interest, each makes a small white love dart. The two snails then fire their love darts into each other's body.

After mating, the snails go their separate ways. In a few weeks, *both* will be ready to lay eggs. So before long, a new generation of snails will be ready to hatch.

Both snails may lay up to forty eggs in the ground.

Every snail's shell has three layers. The grainy, hard part that you see on the outside is a horny layer, and this covers a thinner, chalky layer underneath. Right inside the shell is the third

These are covered with soil and remain hidden there until the babies are born. The baby snails then eat their eggshells, which are highly nutritious. (Snails go through a larval stage *before* hatching because snail larvae are not able to survive outside the eggs.)

mother-of-pearl layer, which is also known as the nacre.

Fossilized snails show that these creepy-crawlies have existed on Earth for 400 million years or more, and that they were among the first creatures to inhabit our planet.

Record-breakers

Next time you find some snails, why not organize a race and check if one would perhaps break a world record!

The smallest snail known, *Punctum pygmeum*, would fit on a pin head with room to spare. But the largest land snail, the Great African snail, *Achaitina*, usually has a shell at least 6in (15cm) high.

According to the *Guinness Book of Records*, one snail from Sierra Leone in West Africa, given the amusing pet name Gee-Geronimo, grew to 15.5in (39.3cm) from head to tail, and weighed a hefty 2lb (900 grams). In Britain, the edible (when cooked) Roman snail has been known to have a shell 4in (10cm) high.

The fastest garden snail and the world record-holder for speed was one called Archie, owned by a young British boy named Carl Bramham.

In July 1995, Archie covered a 13in (32.5cm) course in two minutes. At this speed, Archie would take just over a week to crawl a mile!

Amazingly, there is also a world record for eating the most snails. One man, from La Plata, Maryland, in the U.S., swallowed 350 snails in 8 minutes, 29 seconds. He probably had terrible indigestion!

FACTFILE

Cetain types of snails sometimes attack and eat other snails, even drilling a hole in the shell to get at the victim's soft parts.

World of the snail

- If you go into a restaurant in France, or one elsewhere that serves French food, you may see the dish *escargots* on the menu. This is French for snails. They are boiled in their shells and laced with hot garlic butter. Only the soft body is eaten. Do you find the idea of eating snails tempting?

Slugs

Slugs, like snails, belong to the gastropod group. They look just like snails without their shells. Some, though, have a tiny shell on their backs, or even inside their bodies.

Even peskier in the garden than snails, slugs feed on all sorts of plants and flowers. You can see them sometimes, scraping away at leaves or stems, and maybe roots, too, with their tongue that, like a snail's, is called a radula.

Some slugs are even meat-eaters, burrowing underground to catch earthworms and then sucking them up, just as you might eat a strand of spaghetti, if you fail to wind it around your fork in the correct way!

STRETCHING OUT

Slugs are dull in color – usually brown, black, off-white, gray or yellow. Some may have patterns on their skin, however. In the same way as snails, slugs will also use their muscles to stretch out their bodies at times, and will then shrink them back again. Not having the restrictions of a large shell,

FACTFILE

All slugs and snails are hermaphrodites, and produce round transparent eggs that are often found on compost heaps.

they are also able to wriggle their way along and enter crevices into which a snail, with its large backpack, would never fit.

They, too, hate hot weather but can produce a layer of mucus that will prevent them from drying out if it gets very warm – in fact, it is just as if they had a way of excreting their own sun-screen protection with a high SPF.

This sticky slime has an unpleasant taste to a slug's main enemies – birds, badgers, and frogs. But slugs may also be threatened by other predators, such

as centipedes and even other carnivorous slugs. These may try to eat their eggs. If, however, an enemy approaches, some types of slugs will actively retaliate by squirting mucus directly at the trouble-maker.

Slugs can do considerable damage to plants and crops, which is why horticulturalists and farmers often put down slug pellets to keep them away.

SLUG-SPOTTING

If, by chance, you would like to keep a few slugs for a while to study their behavior, it is easy to set up a fish tank as a temporary home for them. Make sure that you put a layer of gravel for drainage under some damp soil on the bottom of the tank or terrarium, and add some stones, which the slugs can use for shelter, as well as a few small plants and perhaps a little grass.

Place the tank away from the sun and be sure to keep the environment damp. The lid can be made of gauze or netting to provide adequate ventilation.

World of the slug

- A good way to study a slug's mouthparts and eating habits is to place one on a piece of glass with some food. You can then watch from underneath.

- Just like snails, slugs will hibernate in winter when there is less food available for them to eat.

The best time to look for slugs is at night, and after it has rained, with a flashlight. For safety's sake, take along an adult in your family. Encourage the slugs to walk on to a piece of cardboard which you can then drop carefully into your tank. You will, of course, need to feed your slugs regularly, with plants or fruit. Then, after a couple of days, release them once more exactly where you first found them, so that they can return to their natural habitat.

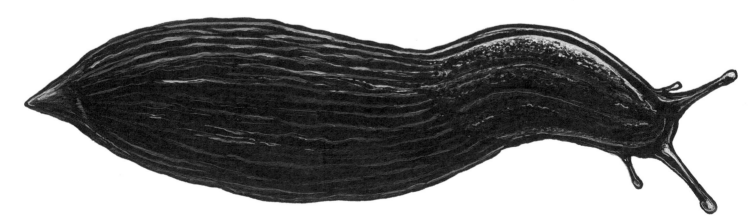

Beetles

Beetles come in all shapes and sizes. Some are no bigger than the period at the end of this sentence. Others, like the Goliath beetle illustrated here and named after the biblical giant, grow to 6in (15cm) in length.

There are so many creatures lining up to eat beetles that they have developed a coat of heavy, bony armor to protect their soft insides.

Like all insects, the beetle has a head, a thorax or chest, and an abdomen. Look at the jaws, known as mandibles, on this one's head! They are strong and powerful. In fact, there are three pairs. Beetles use two pairs for holding their food. They then bite and chew their food with the third set.

Most beetles have quite good eyesight, but rely more on their antennae for feeling their way around. These are on the sides of their heads.

The thorax houses the beetle's heart and is

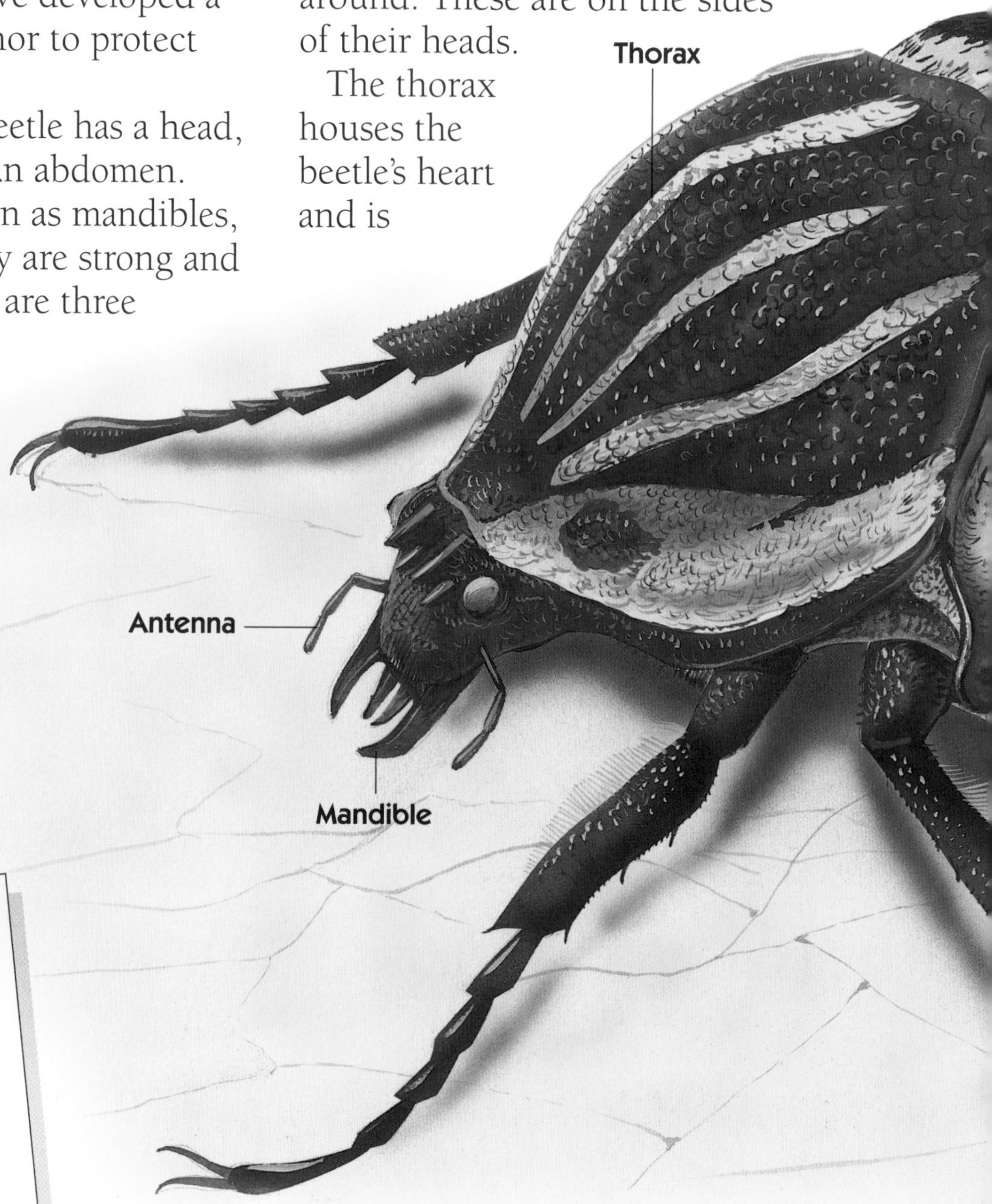

Thorax

Antenna

Mandible

FACTFILE

So-called bloody-nosed beetles will squirt blood from glands in their snouts at the approach of an enemy.

protected by a tough plate called the pronotum.

The abdomen contains the stomach, bowel and breathing system.

Many beetles have two pairs of wings. Those that can fly have a second pair

World of the beetle

● Beetles can be found in all sorts of environments, ranging from the hottest deserts and the thickest tropical forests to the frozen North.

Wing case

that lie beneath the shell-like ones.

The top pair are hard and bony, and called wing-cases, or elytra. They protect the delicate, fan-like wings beneath, which the beetle unfolds when it wants to fly. Beetles have six legs, as do all insects. They are attached to the thorax. Not being able to fly is not always a problem because beetles that cannot fly often have long legs that are useful for running, or strong ones for digging.

Beetle blood tastes awful. Some can even bleed deliberately when attacked, so that the predator won't bother them again. And some will squirt poison.

Fighting over females

A wrestling match between two male Stag beetles is an extremely dramatic event. One may even pick up the other and drop him back down on the ground viciously.

Found in forested areas throughout Europe, Stag beetles live under logs or bark – a very convenient site because their larvae can feed on the wood. When mature, they can also enjoy the tree sap, flowers, and leaves in this environment.

REPELLING INVADERS

Within the forest, each male Stag beetle has his own territory and will mate with all the females in that area. If another male should dare to encroach, however, he will immediately attack the invader, using his large, claw-like mandibles.

The two will now swing punches, like heavyweight boxers do, and knock each other over. One may even cause injury

to the other during this jousting, but neither is likely to be killed. Either beetle may become injured, though, if the battle leaves its shell in any way damaged.

Wing case

Antenna

World of the beetle

- If you ever find a Screech Beetle, you will recognize it by its prominent eyes and also because it squeaks, like a mouse, if disturbed.

Eventually, the weaker beetle gives in and moves away, leaving the other beetle as victor. He now mates with all the females.

BIG DIFFERENCES

Although not as large as the males, which usually measure about 4in (10cm) in length, female Stag beetles have mandibles that are smaller yet even stronger than those of the males, and are particularly useful for getting at food. In fact, male and female Stag beetles look so unalike in many respects that they almost seem to belong to entirely different species.

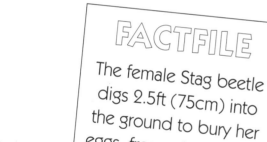

FACTFILE

The female Stag beetle digs 2.5ft (75cm) into the ground to bury her eggs, from which larvae will emerge and dig their way to the surface.

Female

Scientists have discovered that the males of certain types of Stag beetle also use their mandibles for holding onto the females while they mate. Indeed, it may be that the females are actually attracted to the males because of the large antler-like mandibles that give Stag beetles their name.

SLOW DEVELOPERS

Stag beetles live most of their lives developing from larvae into mature adults. After the female has laid her eggs, a tiny grub or larva soon hatches from each one. At this stage, however, the insect looks much more like a worm than the mature adult beetle it will eventually become.

The larvae then take from three to five years to reach adult size. Once they have reached maturity, however, the adult Stag beetle lives only for a short period – just a few months.

Adult Stag beetles have large hind wings, but they do not fly very often, if at all, and you will usually only ever see one in the air at night.

BEETLE-JUICE

In medieval times, people believed the Stag beetle could cure certain illnesses. Juice obtained from boiling beetles in water was even thought – mistakenly, of course – to cure small children of bed-wetting!

The bad and the good

Some beetles do great harm, either indoors or outdoors. Others, however, are very useful to the human population.

Any beetles you find in the house are usually up to no good. They have probably come in for food – *yours*! The larder beetle, for instance, lives up to its name. It will settle into your food cupboard and munch its way through any cold meat that may have been carelessly left uncovered.

Carpet beetles, meanwhile, may lay their eggs in tufts of wool, and the hatching larvae will then gobble up enough of the carpet to ruin it.

Adult furniture beetles are no better. They bore holes into wood to lay their eggs. These hatch into woodworms, which chew their way out. Luckily, special chemicals are available to kill these pests.

PLANT ATTACK

Outdoors, too, we may still not be safe from beetles. Some can demolish the hardiest of plants. Weevils, for example, will lay their eggs inside the stalks of vegetation, which the larvae then eat when they hatch.

Boll weevils live on cotton plants, and can munch their way very quickly through a field. You can read more about them on page 180.

But many beetles actually help keep the garden free from other pests. Ladybugs – a type of beetle – are particularly welcome in the garden because they eat greenflies by the dozen. Meet them on pages 22-23.

FEEDING ON DUNG

Carrion beetles bury dead animals and eat away the rotting flesh, thereby stopping disease from spreading. Dung beetles, meanwhile, as you can see in the illustration *right*, will roll bits of animal droppings into balls and bury them in the ground. This gets rid of the dung and also helps to fertilize the soil.

There are even male and female dung beetles that work in partnership. The female does most of the work, digging a tunnel under the dung – a cow pie, perhaps. The male then brings the dung down to the female.

World of the beetle

- One nocturnal beetle can secrete a substance that will cripple its own offspring, but why it sometimes resorts to this remains a mystery.

She will now push bits of it into specially-built chambers. In each of these, she will lay a single egg. Moving an enormous cow pie is very hard work; but both the male and female stag beetles can feed on the dung for energy, and so will the greedy larvae, when they hatch eventually.

We should be grateful to these dung beetles because, all over the world, hundreds of tons of excrement is disposed of by them underground. Certain types of African dung beetle have even been introduced into Australia, specifically for this purpose.

Sexton or burying beetles, on the other hand, will bury the dead carcasses of small creatures, such as mice or voles, providing food both for themselves and for their larvae in this way.

FACTFILE

Entomologists agree that no other group of insects comes in such dazzlingly different varieties as the beetles, or *Coleoptera*.

Beetle beliefs

Would you believe that a beetle could have great powers? The ancient Egyptians did, worshipping the scarab beetle as a god. They even thought that it rolled the sun round the sky.

A great many superstitions have been associated with beetles over the millennia. Today, too, some African peoples still believe beetles have magical powers. There is one tribe, for example, that throws thousands of beetles into a lake as part of rain-making ceremonies.

Beetles and bad weather seem to go together. In Germany, if you saw a Stag beetle, it once meant a thunderstorm threatened. This was perhaps because stag beetles like to feed on tall oak trees, which are often struck down in storms.

CURE-ALLS?

But should you suck a beetle to cure toothache? Do not even try – it does not work! Hundreds of years ago, though, people did so, because they thought decaying teeth were caused by worms burrowing in the teeth. Some beetles, such as the enlarged violin beetle, *below*, eat worms, so people would pop one in their mouths to try to get rid of the worms and the pain. Not surprisingly, the toothache remained.

FACTFILE

In some parts of the world, highly colored beetles are worn as jewelry – talismans to produce good luck.

Another old custom was to put a beetle, like the rhinoceros beetle, *above*, on to a child's neck to cure whooping cough. This did not work either; but if the child got better, people thought the beetle had been effective. Meanwhile, all this really did was frighten the child.

The powerful Medici family in Italy actually used the ground-up bodies of the Spanish fly beetle to poison their enemies in medieval times. Its blood is highly poisonous and a single drop can make you very sick.

There is even an ancient tale that Jesus was betrayed by a burrowing beetle whose trail revealed the route taken during the flight into Egypt. However, a dung beetle is said to have shown Jesus' enemies another route that was false, so they were led astray.

World of the beetle

- Centuries ago, in Arabia, a beetle that was the same sex as that of a runaway slave would be tied to a nail. The slave-owners believed that this would bring back the slave but, of course, it was just a superstition. If the slave did come back, either captured or of his or her own accord, it was pure coincidence!

Worms

Worms live all around the world, beneath the water and in the earth. At least 1,800 different types exist; and many of these slithery creatures provide essential nutrients for the soil.

You might think that there is nothing much to the body of a earthworm. It doesn't have any bones and nothing that might be called a face – just a mouth at the more pointed end, but no ears, no eyes, no nose. If, however, you look at one closely, you'll soon come to realize that there is a lot more to a worm than first meets the eye.

First of all, you will find that a worm's body is always smooth and slimy. It needs to be moist because this helps it breathe through its skin, which has very fine bristles on the underside.

Most earthworms have bodies that are divided into segments. Every segment, except for the first and the last, has four pairs of these bristles. They help the worm to grip as it moves, pushing itself along by contracting its muscles, segment by segment. If you watch one moving, you'll see that it gets thinner in parts, and then fatter again, as it progresses.

In the middle of the worm, there is a thick, pink section called a saddle. This is used when worms mate. Worms are hermaphrodites – the

scientific term for being both male and female at the same time. When they mate, their saddles meet and are held together by a sticky substance that their bodies make. Later, when the worms separate, they *both* lay eggs in a little brown cocoon – about 0.2in (0.5cm) long.

Earthworms are known as *Annelids* by scientists. This word comes from the Latin for "a ring," and is used to describe their bodies, which are divided into segments or rings.

SENSITIVE CREATURES

Although it has no eyes or ears, the earthworm is not helpless. It knows when it is near the top of the ground, for instance, because the front part of its body can detect even a slight change in light. It can also feel the very smallest vibration on the surface of the soil above it. In fact, your footsteps must seem like thunder to a worm!

World of the worm

- Scientists have estimated that, in a large field of twenty cows, there could be many millions of worms in the soil beneath.

Life underground

Every time you walk through a park or field, remember that there is a whole world of activity going on under your feet as thousands of wriggly earthworms burrow about.

Beneath the soil, there is a strange, dark realm in which millions of earthworms are busy feeding and reproducing. If only you could shrink and travel underground, you could witness their bustling world. You can only see worms during the day if you are digging, because they are night creatures. Too much ultra-violet light kills them.

World of the worm

- You may like to consider building your own glass-sided wormery at home, so you can study the behavior of worms close-up. It is easy to set up, as shown on page 124, and the worms will soon get busy making tunnels.

During the day, they mostly stay deep underground. Only when it is dark do they climb to the top and search for food, poking their heads out above the surface unless, of course, someone starts digging and they are disturbed.

FEEDING TIME

Worms feed on plant materials, and they particularly like decaying leaves, which they either pull into their burrow or place over the entrance for protection and to keep out the sun. Having dragged their food back to a small chamber, they will then cover it with digestive juices, making it soft and ready to eat.

Worms are always burrowing and creating a network of tunnels, the walls of which are strengthened with a sticky substance that comes from the worms' own skin.

They may not look very strong, but these creatures are tougher than you might imagine. If they come to a particularly hard patch of soil, they can continue burrowing by eating their way through it. The soil passes through their bodies and is then deposited behind them in casts, which are very good for the earth. You can see examples of such casts in the illustration *below*.

In fact, worms play an important role in getting flowers and crops to flourish. Their tunnels help water to reach the roots of plants. They also produce nutrient-rich droppings after eating dead leaves. The soil then gradually becomes more fertile.

FACTFILE

Many types of worms have a remarkable ability to mend themselves if they are accidentally wounded by someone digging.

Living off a host

Some types of worm are parasites – living off other creatures – and may be found inside the bodies of certain hosts.

Not all worms are helpful creatures that live in the soil in gardens and fields. Some actually live *inside* other creatures! Being used like this can sometimes be very damaging for the animal that unknowingly plays host to the worm.

There are two main types of parasite worms – tapeworms and roundworms. Tapeworms can enter a host – human or animal – through infected meat. They then use their suckers to attach themselves to the intestine, stealing the food meant for the creature in which they are living. So if you were unlucky enough to get a tapeworm, you would constantly feel hungry and get thinner and thinner.

Roundworms, meanwhile, may live in the gut or even the lungs, kidneys, or eyes. If they grow large, they can make you very ill.

Other parasitic worms, however, do little damage. The ragworm is known to move in and share the shell of a hermit crab, for example, as shown here, cleaning it out like a living vacuum cleaner.

Other worms may have a variety of hosts in their lifetime. The trematode, for example – a wormlike bug – lives part of its life inside a snail, and subsequently lives inside a bird if the snail is then eaten by one, as snails frequently are.

FACTFILE

The sperm whale tapeworm can grow to over 65ft (20m) long – surely a record in the world of parasitic worms!

Observing worms

Worms are very strong creatures for their size. They have no legs, yet are able to move along very easily. In fact, they can burrow through the hardest ground and even push things many times heavier than they are. Yet they have many enemies.

If you would like to study worms closely, you might consider building your own wormery. You could use a glass case or tank, or even an ordinary glass jar that is empty. Cover the top with dark paper, into which you should punch a few airholes – your worms will need to breathe to stay alive. But worms do not like the light, so you should also wrap some dark paper around the jar or case, and remove it when you want to observe your worms as they tunnel.

Use at least two different types of soil, and fill your container in alternating layers. Place some dead or decaying leaves on top of the soil. This will provide your worms with something to eat. Every few days, remember to add a few more leaves. Look for worms for your wormery when it is damp and mild. Place them carefully at the top of the wormery. They will soon get busy making burrows, and you will notice the layers start to merge as the worms mix up the soil. Later, remember to release your worms back to the wild. Here, however, they will undoubtedly encounter enemies.

JUICY PREY

Many animals find worms tasty. Birds are perhaps the best known; but moles, hedgehogs (like the one shown *left*, seen feasting on a juicy victim), as well as badgers, frogs, foxes, shrews, and fish all eat them, too. Pollution, especially in the sea, can also be harmful to worms that live in the water.

World of the worm

- Worms can vary enormously in size and coloring. One found in South America was measured and found to be 22ft (7m) long!

can grow up to 6in (15cm) in length. Velvet worms have a very special way of catching their food. They can squirt a very sticky saliva from their mouths; and while their prey struggle to escape, the velvet worms crawl up to them and start to feed.

Because their bodies do not have any segments, as you can see *top left*, flatworms – in spite of their name – are not classed by entomologists as true worms. Some live in water; others on land; and many actually eat worms of other kinds.

Lugworms and ragworms in particular are very popular with fishermen, who will use them as bait. Placed on a hook, the worms will wriggle, catch the eye of fish, and lure them to the line.

WALKING WORMS

Some worms have ways of coping with predators. Also known as velvet worms, walking worms, like the one in the illustration *bottom right* and on the cover of this book, have bristly bodies with up to 43 pairs of clawed legs. They live under vegetation, squeezing between logs and stones in warm parts of the world, such as South Africa, as well as South and Central America, and

Centipedes

You will often find centipedes if you are gardening, because they rest deep in damp ground or in cool places. But they will come out at night to feed, when you are safely in bed.

The word *centipede* means, literally, "one hundred legs." But the vast majority of these creatures do not actually have that many legs.

The body of a centipede is divided into a number of segments, as you can see here, and each segment contains one pair of legs. Most centipedes have between 15 and 23 such segments; and this, of course, means they will have between 30 and 46 legs.

The most important of all these legs is the front pair, which the centipede uses to grab its prey. They function as claws and are sometimes described as fangs because they bite firmly into a centipede's victim and inject it with a deadly venom.

In some types of centipede, the back legs also act like antennae, and the centipede can use them efficiently to sense its surroundings.

World of the centipede

- One type of centipede from southern Europe, although not very long, has an incredible 177 pairs of legs. That means a total of 354 legs in all!

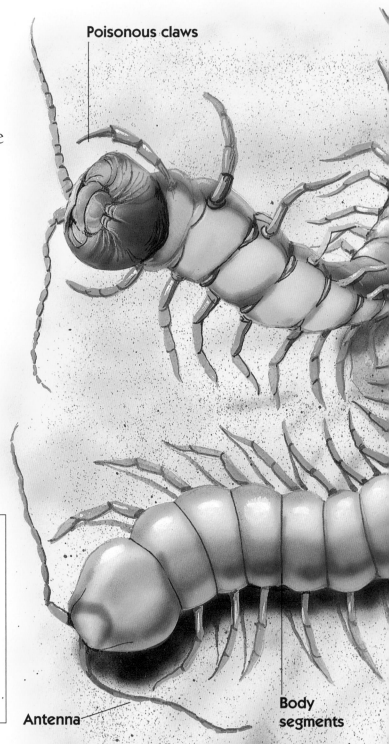

Poisonous claws

Antenna

Body segments

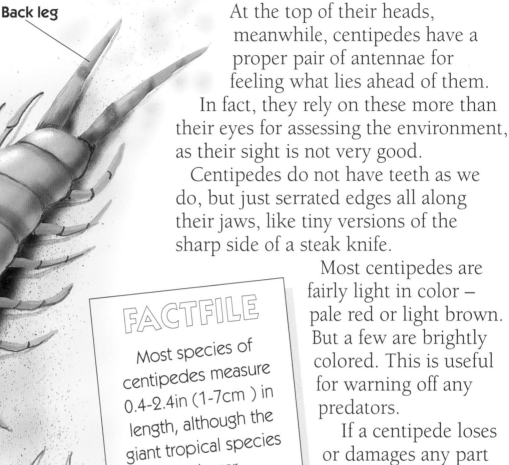

Back leg

WITH FEELING

At the top of their heads, meanwhile, centipedes have a proper pair of antennae for feeling what lies ahead of them.

In fact, they rely on these more than their eyes for assessing the environment, as their sight is not very good.

Centipedes do not have teeth as we do, but just serrated edges all along their jaws, like tiny versions of the sharp side of a steak knife.

Most centipedes are fairly light in color – pale red or light brown. But a few are brightly colored. This is useful for warning off any predators.

If a centipede loses or damages any part of its body – such as its venomous front claws – that part may regrow. But it may be smaller than it was before the accident occurred.

MANY ENEMIES

Centipedes reach maturity after about two years, and can live to the age of seven. Some tropical species have even been known to live for as long as nearly ten years. Their main enemies include lizards, salamanders, shrews, owls, wild cats and even other centipedes, since they can be cannibalistic.

> **FACTFILE**
>
> Most species of centipedes measure 0.4-2.4in (1-7cm) in length, although the giant tropical species are larger.

127

Do not disturb!

The existence of centipedes is a somewhat secluded one, and they hate to be disturbed, as in this picture.

There is nothing a centipede likes more than to settle down for the day in some dark, damp place.

The ideal environment will be beneath stones, among twigs or tree bark, or under clumps of dead leaves. If you lift up a stone or uncover some leaf mold, you might find quite a few of them. But it is best to leave them where they are, because they do not like being disturbed. If, by accident, you do disturb them, you will probably find that they quickly scuttle away to some other secluded retreat among leaf litter.

They prefer to rest during the day and hunt by night, attacking flies, ants, earthworms, and larvae. Some giant centipedes even rear up off the ground and snatch bees and wasps from out of the air! When it is hot, they will burrow deep into the ground to find cool, damp earth – a more comfortable environment for them.

But if the soil is waterlogged, they will come to the surface to escape being drowned. These fussy creatures do not like the soil to be too tightly packed either. This would prevent them from burrowing through it easily.

Some centipedes have special glands in the back segments of their bodies that contain extraordinary chemicals. These will light up their bodies, creating a marvelous glow. However, they only do this if they are disturbed.

World of the centipede

- The house centipede, common in North America, is about 1.2in (3cm) long with 15 pairs of thin legs and distinctive stripes along its back.

Predatory mini-beasts

For creatures of their size, centipedes are remarkable predators, chasing after their prey with extraordinary speed.

Once night starts to fall, a centipede will prepare to go hunting for food. And what a lot of food this energetic little creature likes to eat! So it is just as well that it can wriggle along so quickly, using its many muscular legs to chase something for its dinner. It can even turn corners at good speed, although even experts have always found it hard to tell in which order a centipede moves all its legs as it performs this feat.

MINI-PREDATORS

Centipedes are, in fact, very well suited to the role of predator, with front legs that double as fanged claws. Once they sink these into their prey, there is little chance of escape for their miniature victims. The claws contain a venom that is lethal to insects, such as the beetle shown here. The fangs of giant centipedes even contain enough venom to kill bigger creatures, such as lizards. There are also times when centipedes, if extremely hungry, become cannibals and will eat others of their own kind!

Some centipedes also have special glands in their segmented bodies. If these centipedes happen to be under attack, the glands will release a sticky, poisonous substance.

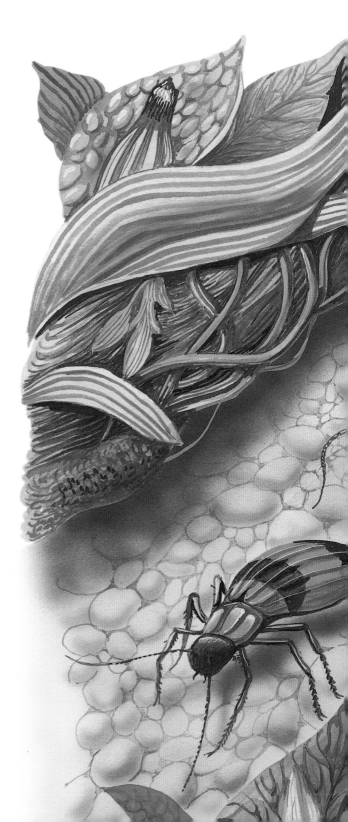

World of the centipede

- Centipedes have a large appetite, ridding the land of many pests, such as the weevil; so, on the whole, they are very useful.

But other creatures are forewarned. They know that this type of centipede is dangerous because it is usually brightly-colored.

Most centipedes are harmless to humans, and will not attack unless provoked; but the venom of the giant centipedes that live in tropical climates can be dangerous. A bite from one of these will cause an intense burning pain, and the resulting swelling may last for many hours.

Centipedes feed on spiders, worms, toads, beetles, and small snakes, but they are sometimes themselves the prey of other creatures. They are even used by fishermen in the Far East as bait.

LEG COUNT

Most centipedes have under one hundred legs. In fact, they can never be true to their name and have exactly one hundred legs because they always have an odd number of body segments. With two legs to a segment, it is impossible to reach the exact figure of one hundred.

Birth of a centipede

After mating, male and female centipedes split up, leaving the females to care for the young.

Centipedes are born in one of two ways, according to the species to which they belong. Some are born whole, with all their legs intact. Others hatch with just seven pairs of legs. They then add more as they mature and develop more body segments.

Mating occurs after a long courtship dance. The male and female centipedes circle each other for several minutes, as shown here, before the males leave small packets of seeds on the ground nearby. The females pick these seeds up and proceed to use them to fertilize their eggs.

The female centipede likes to lay her eggs in the summer and puts a lot of effort into giving birth to her babies. In many species, the mother will build a small mound out of mud, making an indentation in the top, in which she will then lay her eggs.

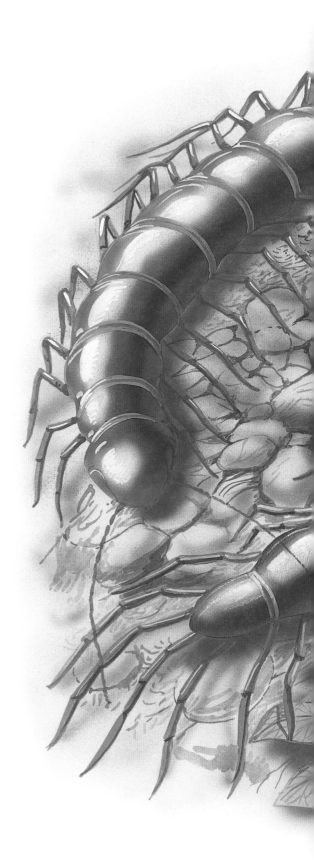

World of the centipede

- It has been calculated that, in under just one acre (0.4 hectares) of ground, there could be as many as 38 million centipedes.

While waiting for them to hatch, she will coil her body around the mound for protection.

In other species, after laying her eggs, the female will roll them along the ground. Because the eggs are sticky, little particles of earth soon become attached to them. Safely disguised as lumps of soil, they will be free from the attention of other animals, and so have more chance of survival. The eggs are then left to hatch.

EXCELLENT MOTHERS

Female centipedes make fine parents. While waiting for their eggs to hatch, they take good care of them, protecting them from scavengers and even giving them an occasional cleaning. Once the babies have hatched, the mothers continue to look after them, giving them food and staying nearby until they can fend for themselves. They have even been known to lick their babies to keep them clean.

While centipedes are still growing to their eventual full length, they shed their outer skin at regular intervals. This molting normally takes place during the hours of darkness. Each process of molting can take an hour or two. It takes two years for a centipede to reach full maturity, by which time it will itself begin to breed.

FACTFILE

The biggest centipede known is found in the Bay of Bengal area of India and measures all of 13in (33cm) in length.

Millipedes

They may be tiny, but millipedes are great diggers, and you may well come across them if you do some gardening and turn over the soil.

Take a good look at the creatures illustrated on the opposite page. At first, they may seem similar to each other. Once you start to study them more closely, however, you will find they are not entirely alike. Some are centipedes and others are millipedes; and there are several differences between the two types of creatures.

Millipedes, as their name meaning "one thousand legs" suggests, have more legs than centipedes, but not literally one thousand – usually 40-400. There are four (two pairs) on most segments of their bodies. But, strangely, the longest millipedes do not have the most legs, as not all segments are the same size.

Centipedes have just two legs, or one pair, on each body segment. However, centipedes move much more quickly than millipedes, which are sluggish in comparison. But, then, centipedes need to move quickly because they are carnivorous, and always on the hunt for insects and worms. Millipedes, meanwhile, tend to live mainly on decaying plants. Their coloring is different, too. Millipedes are usually darker than centipedes.

ROLLING UP

Millipedes do not have venomous claws like centipedes, but some types do have poisonous glands in their skin to deter attackers. Otherwise, unlike the more aggressive centipede, they will curl up into a ball until any threat disappears. During this time, the shells covering each segment of their bodies overlap to form a sort of protective armor.

Centipedes are useful because they will control harmful insects. Some millipedes, however, will damage plants so they are classed as pests. What is more, most millipedes stink! In fact, if there are lots in a field, the smell of them can make you feel sick.

There are more than 3,000 types of centipedes and around 6,500 types of millipedes. Can you now tell which are which on the *opposite* page?

World of the millipede

- Millipedes like to live under rotting logs, together with creatures such as worms, beetles, centipedes, mites, springtails, wood lice, and false scorpions. Here, they can enjoy an environment that is both warm and moist, and they will be fairly safe from a number of potential predators.

Now that you know how many legs a millipede has on each section of its body, can you calculate how many legs a millipede with thirty-one sections to its body must have?

(The answer should be 124, which you get if you multiply the number of segments by 4.)

Cockroaches

Smooth-backed, long-legged, and terribly greedy, cockroaches love warm places where there is lots of food. They may be hard to get rid of, if they appear in your kitchen.

Most people are revolted by the sight of a cockroach. But even if you have never before seen one in real life, you will easily recognize these pests. They vary in size; but the common cockroach – also known as the "black beetle" – is, for example, around 1in (23mm) long.

QUIVERING ANTENNAE

You will know them at once by the two very long, thin, many-jointed antennae situated at the front of their heads. These seem to be constantly quivering. Although cockroaches have good eyesight, they need their antennae to help them feel around for things and for sniffing out scraps. At the other end of their bodies, they have what looks like another, but much shorter, pair of antennae, too, called cerci.

A cockroach's six legs are long and spiky. Notice, too, how their flat bodies are covered by what seems to be a sort of leathery protective shield.

MULTI-COLORED

The most common types of cockroach include the "black beetle" and the 0.5in (1cm)-long German cockroach (in spite of its name, not originally from Germany) which is striped and a yellow-brown color.

Wing buds

Compound eye

World of the cockroach

- There are well over 3,000 different types of cockroaches. They seem to be present wherever the environment is warm and there is food.

Most magnificent of all is the reddish-brown American cockroach. It is three times as long as the German cockroach at 1.5in (4cm) and, again, not originally from where its name suggests.

Some species of cockroaches have no wings at all, while others just have two pairs of tiny flaps for wings. Where there are two pairs of wings, the males' wings are larger. In a number of cockroaches, however, the wings are more fully developed; but cockroaches still hardly ever take to the air, preferring life on the ground, so you will hardly ever see one in flight.

A cockroach's head is often hidden under the thorax or middle part of its body. If you could look at one under a microscope, you would see that this greedy creature's jaws and many teeth are ideal for chewing.

CONTAMINATORS

Cockroaches will feed on any scraps that they can find if they manage to invade a kitchen; but in the wild, they exist mainly on animal remains, even of their own kind, although they would not kill another cockroach for a meal.

What makes cockroaches most detestable is that they carry disease, and so can very easily contaminate any food that they happen to touch.

Cerci

Antenna

FACTFILE

Cockroaches were around in prehistoric times and may have eaten scraps of dead flesh that were left by dinosaurs.

Hungry encroachers

There are lots of household items that cockroaches will make a meal of; but could these pests possibly have their uses?

Cockroaches love the environment of a not-too-clean kitchen. But this is not just because there is more chance of finding food there than anywhere else in your house or apartment.

These insects originate from tropical parts of the world; and although millions of generations of them may have lived in cooler parts of our planet for many centuries, they will still instinctively seek out warmth.

Amazingly, though, cockroaches are not just partial to leftovers and crumbs of food but will happily eat paper and even fabric of all kinds, including leather. In fact, they have been known to chew their way through book-bindings; and, strange as it may seem, they like shoe polish and ink, too.

So watch out for your jacket, sneakers and jeans, as well as any leftover food, if any cockroaches have been spotted in your home!

MINIATURE SPIES

However, it seems that cockroaches can possibly be of some use. Japanese scientists have recently developed remote-controlled cockroaches by grafting microchips on to the backs of live specimens. Equipped with mini-cameras, these tiny bionic creatures may become spies of the future! Just imagine – they might, for instance, be sent in to photograph secret documents...unless, of course, they are stepped on before they have a chance to complete their mission!

World of the cockroach

- Scientists have developed a way to protect our homes from these creatures. Special traps release a scent that is attractive to cockroaches. Once they are aware of it, they are then lured to their deaths.

FACTFILE

Cockroaches are very fast runners on their long, slim legs, and are notoriously difficult to catch when they are found in the home.

Hatching out

Ther majority of females of these detested insects are not caring mothers, abandoning the larvae before they have even had a chance to hatch from their eggs.

Take a look at this German cockroach. It must be a female. How can you tell? There is one important clue in the picture *below* – the fact that she is carrying a tiny brown purse attached to the back of her body.

or so later, she will deposit it into a crevice or crack. Then the females of most species of cockroach abandon it. From now on, they take no interest at all in their offspring, making rather poor parents. Their babies become orphans.

A cockroach's purse usually has two rows of eggs, eight in each row, with a separate pocket for each. The sixteen eggs will hatch about eight weeks later. But some types of cockroaches have an ootheca containing more than twice as

It is not a real purse, of course, and has no money in it! But the purse – or ootheca, as scientists call it – does contain something of value for future generations of cockroaches – the female's eggs!

For the moment, the female carries her purse around all the time. But a day

many eggs. In species where lots of eggs are produced, the mothers are a little more caring, however, and carry their purses until just before the larvae hatch. The young secrete a form of saliva that softens the ootheca so that its sides will

World of the cockroach

- Some cockroaches make odd hissing sounds to scare off a predator.

shed their skin several times, as shown in this illustration strip, and darken.

Development into adults may take as long as a year, but it is easy to see how rapidly a cockroach colony can grow, if the mothers go on laying at least sixteen eggs at a time! Some cockroaches are specially bred in zoos and universities so that researchers can learn more

separate and the larvae can finally begin to emerge.

Some types of cockroaches, however, do not carry their eggs in an ootheca at all.

Baby cockroaches are generally white at first and immediately start running here and there. While growing, they

about their behavior. A few, such as the Australian giant cockroaches, are also becoming increasingly rare, so they are bred in captivity for scientific study and to maintain the species in case they become extinct in the wild. Let's hope they don't ever escape and start to invade an Australian kitchen!

Illicit immigrants

Centuries ago, these crafty creatures managed to travel hundreds of miles without moving a muscle.

Insects sometimes reach distant shores by accident. They creep into the cargo holds of ships, or even airplanes, much like human stowaways; and soon they may find themselves in an entirely different country.

This was originally the case with the black beetle cockroach. Lots of these insects, it is said, were brought to England by the renowned sailor Sir Francis Drake. This 16th-century seaman not only circumnavigated the world but also led England's war against the Spanish Armada. He even became a notorious pirate, taking booty from a great many Spanish trading vessels.

One such ship carried sacks of exotic spices. Among these, Drake later found swarms of the dreaded cockroach. So, many of those cockroaches alive in Great Britain or various other parts of the world today could possibly be direct descendants of the cockroaches that once crawled around in Drake's booty or amidst similar cargo on its way to other parts of the world.

GLOBETROTTERS

The German cockroach, meanwhile, also known as the croton bug in the United States, is thought to have been introduced to England when troops returned from the Crimean War in 1856. The German cockroach originated in Asia. It reaches maturity in only a few months, whereas other cockroaches can take several years; and so, in no time at all, there may be enormous swarms of them. Another type comes from Central America, but has travelled widely; and, most extraordinary, some even originate from Lapland!

More recently, the Surinam cockroach has also reached Great Britain, but it is a plant pest and probably does not invade kitchens at all.

World of the cockroach

- Cockroaches become darker and smellier as they molt with maturity. This smell is their means of defense against enemies and is released from two openings located underneath their developing bodies.

Kitchen pests

Health inspectors always look for any evidence of cockroaches when checking on the hygiene of restaurant premises. You will not want them in your home, either.

You will know by now that there is nothing that cockroaches like more than a dirty kitchen. That is why it is so important to keep your home scrupulously clean so that it is free from scraps, and to store all food very carefully. You also need to keep your trash cans clean and disinfected.

World of the cockroach

- A cockroach is the perfect example of an omnivore, a creature that will eat almost anything. In fact, you can be sure that a cockroach will enjoy feeding on whatever you eat or wear. They even like ink and sandpaper!

Air conditioning and ventilation ducts, cracks in the walls or base-boards and the underside of flooring – all these places are likely hiding places for cockroaches by day. They may even lurk there in large numbers. Then, at nightfall, they venture out into the open in search of crumbs.

But cockroaches will actually infect more than they consume, so serious food poisoning can sometimes result if a cockroach has crawled over a plate or dish of food.

STAMPING THEM OUT

If you suspect this, throw the food away. It can be helpful to use an insecticide, if you know where the pests are. But only an adult should ever use an insecticide powder or spray because these can themselves be poisonous and may cause irritation to the skin.

If you see a cockroach, tell an adult. Don't try to

pick it up because of the germs they carry. Besides, they often have sharp spikes on their legs. But if hordes of cockroaches become a real problem in your kitchen or elsewhere in your home, it will be best to call in an environmental health expert or a pest control company.

In the United States, some people who have cockroaches in their homes have even started to keep geckos, as shown in this illustration. They are tropical lizards that sleep by day but come out at night and hunt cockroaches. What an ingenious way of coping with such nasty pests!

UNWELCOME HOUSE GUESTS

Cockroaches, of course, can live just as comfortably out of doors. If ever you happen to find some cockroaches venturing out at dusk – in the garden, for example – and are tempted to take a few home in order to observe them closely, you had better not do so. It is highly possible that they might be females that can lay eggs, and your home could soon become infested with hundreds of these little creatures. This is not a pleasant thought!

FACTFILE

A strange odor in the kitchen at breakfast might be due to a visit from a colony of cockroaches making their home there.

Ants

Some ants are only about 0.08in (2mm) long, while others are giants in comparison, about the length of your little finger. They can be found all over the world, except for frozen wastelands, and all have one thing in common – they live in colonies or large groups.

Next time you have a chance, take a close look at an ant and try to imagine how frightening it must seem to any smaller insect that the ant is planning to attack. As you can see from the much-larger-than-life illustration here, it has quite a big head for its body size. Notice, too, those two stalks growing from its head. These are its antennae and are used for touching, feeling, smelling and tasting. Ants do not have ears like yours, but they can "hear" by detecting vibrations in the ground. Like other insects, ants have compound eyes, with up to 1000 lenses in each, instead of just the one lens that you have in each of yours. Compound eyes are good at spotting movement but can only focus on objects that are very close.

The thorax is behind the ant's head and contains the heart, as well as a passage that carries food from the head to the abdomen. The thorax also contains strong muscles, some of which power the ant's legs.

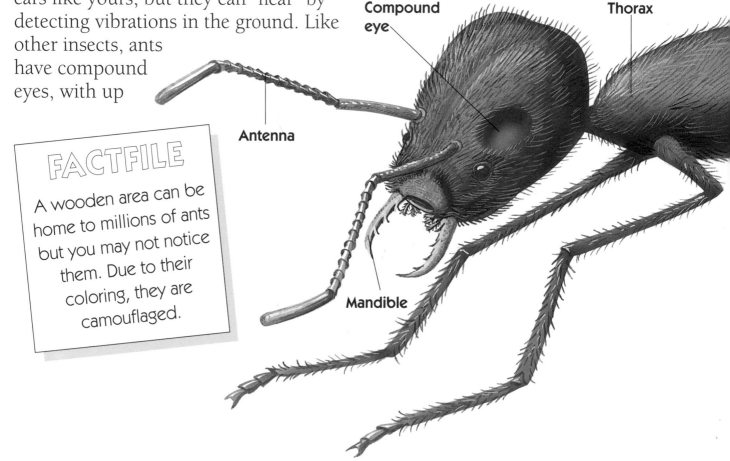

Compound eye

Thorax

Antenna

Mandible

FACTFILE

A wooden area can be home to millions of ants but you may not notice them. Due to their coloring, they are camouflaged.

146

A thin waist connects the thorax to the abdomen, where food is digested. The abdomen is large compared with the tiny thorax. Some ants also have a venomous sting at the back end of the abdomen, with which they defend themselves in case of attack by any one of a number of predatory enemies.

The ant's body is covered with a shell-like skin, known as the exoskeleton. This acts as a kind of suit of armor and is there to protect its internal organs from injury. Males and queens have wings. Other types of ants never have them.

World of the ant

- Worker ants sometimes fight members of other colonies that belong to the same species. They may have fierce, long-lasting battles, and many may be killed before the winners eventually take over the enemy nest.

Petide

Abdomen

ON THE MOVE

A scientist recently calculated that the army ant – 0.4in (1cm) long – can move at 10ft (3m) per minute, which is the equivalent of 0.11mph (0.18km/h).

This may sound slow. But bear in mind that a small family car is about 450 times longer than an ant. Multiply the ant's speed by 450, and you will see that the ant's rate is then the equivalent of about 50mph (80km/h). This is not as fast as a car can go at top speed, but it is still a lot faster than *you* can run!

Some ants move even more quickly over short distances. Scientists estimate, for example, that one type of desert ant from Africa can run at the equivalent of 100mph (160km/h)!

A huge family

You are probably familiar with black ants and may also have seen reddish-brown ones. You may even have spotted yellow ants and ants that fly. But did you know there are in fact thousands of different types?

Amazingly, there are over 10,000 different species of ants – so there is only room to look at a few of them here. One of the most common is the black garden ant. It lives in meadows and forests, as well as in gardens, where it may nest in colonies under stones and logs, or even paved areas. You have probably seen them, crawling around as in the picture shown *below*. They feed on other smaller insects, and milk aphids for honeydew.

If you have ever come across flying ants, they were probably black garden ants, as *above*. As adults, the males and queens, all of which have wings, leave the nest where they were born, in a swarming process known as the "marriage flight." After mating with the queens, the males die.

World of the ant

- The main enemies of ants are birds. But other creatures that enjoy a meal of ants include the South American ant-eater which catches ants (and termites) by poking its long, sticky tongue right into their nests.

Tailor ants, like those from India that you can see *below*, are also known as weaver ants and make a nest from leaves. They pass their larvae to and fro between leaves in a tree. The larvae then spin sticky silk, which holds the leaves together, to form the nest.

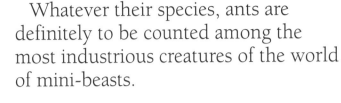

Whatever their species, ants are definitely to be counted among the most industrious creatures of the world of mini-beasts.

South American leaf-cutter ants, such as the one shown *right*, like certain other ants, grow fungus in their nests, which they process for use as food. First, they cut tiny pieces from the leaves of plants close to the nest, and then they haul them home. Once back at the nest, they chew the leaves and spread them around the fungus, as compost.

Life in the colony

Anyone who has ever come across an ant nest will immediately be struck by how extremely busy all the residents are.

Most of the ants in a nest are workers. These are all females that look after the queen, or queens, who lay all the eggs. The workers also care for the larvae that hatch from her eggs.

After a while, the larvae will spin cocoons for themselves and become pupae, as they begin to turn into adult ants. The workers look after these, too.

TO SERVE AND DEFEND

One of the most important tasks of the workers is to collect food for the whole colony of ants. Larger workers, sometimes called soldiers, have another role, however, and must defend the colony if it is attacked. If this happens, all the workers try to save the young. But the soldiers will actually fight back, using their jaws, and also their stingers, if they have them.

Apart from the queen and the workers, there are also young queens and males in the nest. These have wings and will fly away when it is time to mate.

The males' only job is to mate with the queens, who can then lay their own eggs and start a new colony.

An ant nest could not survive unless all the ants worked well together and

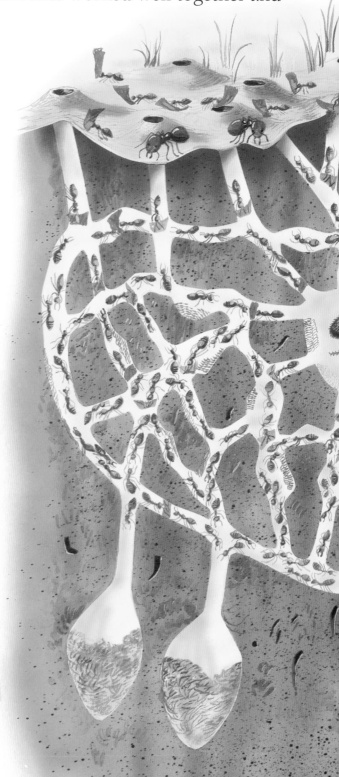

FACTFILE

A few types of ants can sting – among them some red ants, driver ants from Africa, and the army ants of South America.

World of the ant

- Humans have always been fascinated by how hard ants work. There is mention of this in the biblical **Book of Proverbs**, and in a fable by Aesop, a writer from Ancient Greece who wrote exemplary tales, giving advice for life.

communicated. They do this by means of smell. Each nest has its own scent, so that the ants can recognize each other. Ants also use scent trails to guide each other to good sources of food.

The nest shown here belongs to a colony of leaf-cutter ants. Look carefully and see if you can you spot the queen, her eggs, the workers, and the soldiers.

Some ants even share their nests with aphids, providing them with honeydew, mites, white wood lice, and some types of beetles, which the ants may even feed.

DISAPPEARING TRICKS

European wood ants are reddish-brown and live mostly in pine woods, where they are hard to spot, particularly as they will pile pine needles and sticks over their nests. Carpenter ants, meanwhile, are brown - a good color for insects that need to hide in the dark bark of trees. Others, such as yellow meadow ants, live in grassy places and their bodies merge well with the dead, sun-baked grasses that lie on the meadow floors. They, too, are well camouflaged in such an environment. It is very much a case of "now you see them, now you don't."

On the march

Army ants spend the greater part of their lives on the move and will frequently attack.

It is dawn in a South American forest, and there is movement on the ground under the trees. A large colony of stinging army ants is on the march.

These ants spend much of their lives marching by day and resting at night, clustered around their queen, eggs and larvae. Now, as the morning light reaches the forest floor, they begin to form a column about 10ft (3m) wide. The leading ants set off, leaving a trail of scent, and the others follow.

Soldier ants (large workers) stay on the outside of the column to defend it. The queen and other workers, meanwhile, march in the center, carrying the eggs and larvae.

At times, scouts begin to break away from the column to look for food. One group now fans out and swarms quickly over its prey. It is a moth many times larger than the army ants, which sting and smother it to death, as you can see in this illustration.

FACTFILE

As they leave their temporary camps, army ants will use their bodies as bridges to cross difficult terrain.

Others may soon divide into smaller columns, and attack anything vulnerable. The forest now fills with low-level sound, as leaves rustle and other small insects start to buzz in warning that a killer army is invading.

Army ants march every day while the young are still larvae. When the young reach the stage of becoming pupae (prior to full adulthood), however, the ants need less food and so the killer army will settle for a while

ALL CHANGE!

There is no leader to the colony, but army ants have an interesting way of sharing their positions. After a certain amount of time marching, the ants at the front of the column turn around and let others from behind, which are still moving forward, take their place. The column hardly ever stops. Even if any of the ants become separated from the colony for any reason, their fellow marchers simply continue moving and leave them behind.

World of the ant

- Army ants have a killing instinct and will feed on grasshoppers, moths, spiders, and also other types of ants. They have even been known to kill lizards many times their own size.

Fleas

If you notice an animal start to scratch itself, it might have fleas – nasty little bugs just the size of a speck of dust, but with the power to give an animal a painful bite, and to jump to great heights.

Fleas are so small – only about 0.05in (1-10mm) long – that, to study them properly, you need to look at them under a microscope, as we have done here. In fact, some are smaller than a grain of sand or speck of dust. This one has been enlarged a great many times. They are usually brown, which provides excellent camouflage on most animals.

Fleas have no respect at all. They will jump on to animals or people, bite, suck their blood, and run away when a giant paw or hand tries to squash them. They do not have wings but they do not need to fly as such. They simply jump. Some do not even have eyes! Once on the body of a living creature, known as a host, they simply feel their way along.

As you can see, a flea has three main parts to its body: a head, thorax (chest), an abdomen, and also six legs. What is more, its body is so thin that it could have been ironed flat!

The two spikes at the front of a flea's head are the antennae, which are used for feeling; and the longer, fearsome-looking spikes are the mouthparts. These are called stylets and have

jagged, cutting edges, like a steak knife. The flea uses them to bite its host and suck up its blood.

LIKE A CATAPULT

The secret of the flea's jumping power is a hard pad made out of an elastic substance, called resilin, in its thorax. This pad is pulled back like a catapult when the flea bends its back legs. As the legs stretch out,

FACTFILE

Fossils of fleas that have been found in Australia are 200 million years old, so they were living at the same time as the dinosaurs.

Back leg

the pad then straightens up and hurls the flea forward.

The flea's abdomen is covered by ten overlapping bony plates. These will

Compound eye

Mouthparts

protect its soft insides if a creature scratches at it, as it is bound to do because flea bites cause intense irritation. The scratching eventually ruptures the skin, resulting in ugly sores. A flea will survive attempts to squash it unless these plates are broken, when they will make a cracking sound.

World of the flea

● The most dangerous flea in the world is the oriental rat flea that lives on rats and carries such deadly diseases as the plague and typhus fever.

Adult fleas can live for quite a while, providing there is a steady supply of blood to suck. A human flea has even been known to live for nearly 17 years.

BAD BITES

A flea bite first appears as a small red lump as the flea injects its saliva into the victim. It is best not to scratch it.

The world's most popular host for fleas is the red squirrel – as many as thirteen thousand fleas have been discovered on just one! Poultry also often suffer from flea bites.

Most flea bites are harmless. But if a flea has been sucking the blood of a diseased animal and then bites you, it can pass on that disease through the injected saliva.

In general, fleas lead independent lives, as they seek out victims to bite, but they may also live alongside others if food is plentiful. They breed best in warm, dry conditions, although those that inhabit Arctic regions have been able to adapt to sub-zero temperatures.

The flea circus

Can fleas really be taught to perform tricks, tiny as they are? Or is there some sort of optical illusion or deceit involved?

Step right up! We're taking a journey back in time, to a sunny summer day one hundred years ago, and we are off to the fair. You had better get there early, or you won't get a good view of the latest craze – the flea circus. Amazingly, you'll witness tiny fleas that actually seem to race, pull tiny coaches, and perform all sorts of wonderful tricks.

The circus master keeps them in an enclosed sand pit, but sometimes you can only see them when they disturb the dust. This is because the fleas are, of course, only a fraction of an inch (a few millimeters) long. However, we have enlarged them greatly in this illustration so that they can be seen cleanly.

Some flea-circus showmen have fleas that seem to swordfight. Two fleas face each other and have small swords tied to their legs by wire that is finer than your hair. As they wave their legs, the little swords clash.

The showmen say that they spent hours training the fleas, but they are only teasing. You cannot actually train a flea, but you *can* use its natural movements to create what seem to be miniature sporting events. The real skill is in building the coaches and other props, and catching the fleas to tie them down. How amusing it must have been to watch circus fleas running back and forth, tied to little chariots, or performing on a tightrope!

But showmen were not the only people who had to find ways of catching fleas in the past when everyone was not as hygienic as they are today. One ingenious method involved hanging china tubes from the waistband of a lady's wired petticoat worn under her crinoline skirt. The tubes would be filled with honey to which any fleas would be attracted, only to get stuck in the sticky substance. The honey and dead fleas would be scraped out at intervals, and fresh honey was then inserted.

World of the flea

- The most famous scientist to study the behavior of the flea was Dr. Miriam Rothschild. She discovered the importance of resilin, the substance that gives fleas their incredible jumping power, and has over a quarter of a million words about fleas to her name!

Birth of a flea

Follow the strip *below*, and find out how the eggs of a flea develop through the larval stage to maturity, when they start biting.

New fleas come into the world as pearly white eggs, only the size of dots. The female flea mates only once, and will then lay about 25 eggs each day for the rest of her lifespan. This is normally about three or four weeks, so a single flea may finally lay up to 700 eggs in total in her lifetime. You can see some of them greatly enlarged, *below left*, that have been laid on a cat's fur.

After a few days, or sometimes as long as two weeks later, the eggs turn into larvae. These are long, a little like worms, white, and as yet have no eyes or legs. They do not suck blood, but live on any dust and bits of dead skin and dried blood lying around.

As they get older, however, they do start to need fresh blood, which the

World of the flea

• If your cat or dog is found to have fleas, be sure to buy it a flea collar containing substances that kill fleas. These chemicals are very strong, however, so remove the collar if soreness develops around your pet's neck. It will be a good idea to see your vet, too.

mother flea will provide. She does this by passing it out through her bottom – not a very pleasant thought, but nevertheless welcomed by the larvae.

Flea larvae often get shaken out of an animal's fur, to live in its bedding. After two or three weeks, the larvae then weave cocoons around themselves, shed their skin and pupate.

Fleas like warmth, and so developing fleas are able to delay maturing if they sense that the weather is cold.

Then they will start jumping and biting, like the highly magnified ones that are shown *below right.*

If nothing has been done to kill them, the poor cat will be in for a terribly irritating time!

This means pupae that are laid as eggs in winter do not usually hatch until the first sign of spring.

Spreading the plague

Fleas are not only annoying parasites; they can also cause serious illness and even kill if carrying certain infections, although this is much rarer today that it once was.

Drinking a meal of blood might sound disgusting, but adult fleas cannot live on anything else. If there are plenty of animals – or people – around, they usually eat once a day. But if they are unable to find anything suitable, they can go for months without sucking a single drop. When they eventually find a victim, though, they will have a feast.

HOLE-PUNCHERS

Fleas use three razor-sharp points, called stylets, to punch holes in an animal's or a human's skin. Then they spit into the holes, and their saliva shoots down a special tube in the stylets. Now they can begin to suck up some blood.

With luck, they will get enough food to last the day from just one bite. But if their host scratches and interrupts the start of the meal, they will have to bite all over again.

THE BLACK DEATH

Ancestors of today's rat fleas helped to wipe out 25 million people in Europe in the middle of the 14th century, in an outbreak of illness known as the Black Death. While it raged, a quarter of the population of that part of the world died as a result.

The streets at that time, as you can see in the illustration *opposite*, were infected with rats. Their fleas would suck up bubonic plague germs from the rats and then pass them on to humans. Fleas can still pass on diseases today, although people are generally cleaner, and fortunately there are medicines to cure most illnesses.

HUNGRIER AND HUNGRIER

The plague spread very rapidly because most fleas carrying the disease developed a blockage in their digestive system due to the bacteria. Then, when they continued to feed, the blood they took in, as a result of biting, flowed back to the host, and carried with it some of the bacteria. The fleas got hungrier and hungrier because no food got through the blockage, and so they bit even more people, in the attempt to get a meal. Eventually, the flea died.

World of the flea

- Fleas can move with a force several times greater than that necessary to launch a rocket into space!

- There are about 1,400 known species of fleas in the world.

Mantises

When an insect lands to feed on a plant's sweet nectar, a mantis may be ready to make a move and to grab its victim.

Cockroaches are hardly cute! But they do have a relative that is far more charming in appearance. It is the praying mantis.

Study the illustration of an orchid mantis, *right*, one of the praying mantises, and you will soon understand how this insect got its curious name. As you can see, it is standing on only four of its six legs. Its front legs, meanwhile, are held out in front of its face, as if it is praying. But don't be fooled! It is not doing anything so harmless. A hungry predator, it is actually waiting patiently to grab any passing prey which it will do with lightning speed. The mantis is strictly a carnivore and will never eat vegetation, even though often surrounded by it, as you can see here; and what is more, it will eat its prey alive.

CLEVER COLORING

Some mantises are green in color, and perfectly camouflaged among new leaves. Others can be pinkish in color, and, as a result, will be well hidden among blossoms or flowers. They look just like part of the vegetation.

The Indian mantis, however, is colored a particular shade of brown so that it looks like the dead foliage on a forest floor and is practically invisible in its environment.

Such camouflage helps disguise each type of mantis so that it will not be spotted by its prey, nor by enemies such as lizard and birds.

Native to warmer parts of the world only, most mantises can fly but do not often use their wings. Handle one, and it may try to bite you – but it is not venomous. However, when it strikes at a victim, it will spike it with the claws and spines on its legs, and there is little chance of escape.

The mantis has other great physical advantages, too. Its neck is extremely flexible, and so it can twist around to see any creature approaching from the rear. It also has very large, round eyes that protrude from its head, enabling it to have a very wide viewpoint, much wider than ours.

It takes about six months for mantis eggs to hatch; and before they turn into adults, they will also take on a disguise.

World of the mantis

- Male and female mantises look very different. The females are much bigger, and sometimes take advantage of this, by eating their mates.

162

As adults, they will look like plants; but until then, before they start to molt and become mature, they will closely resemble red stinging ants. So potential predators are very wary!

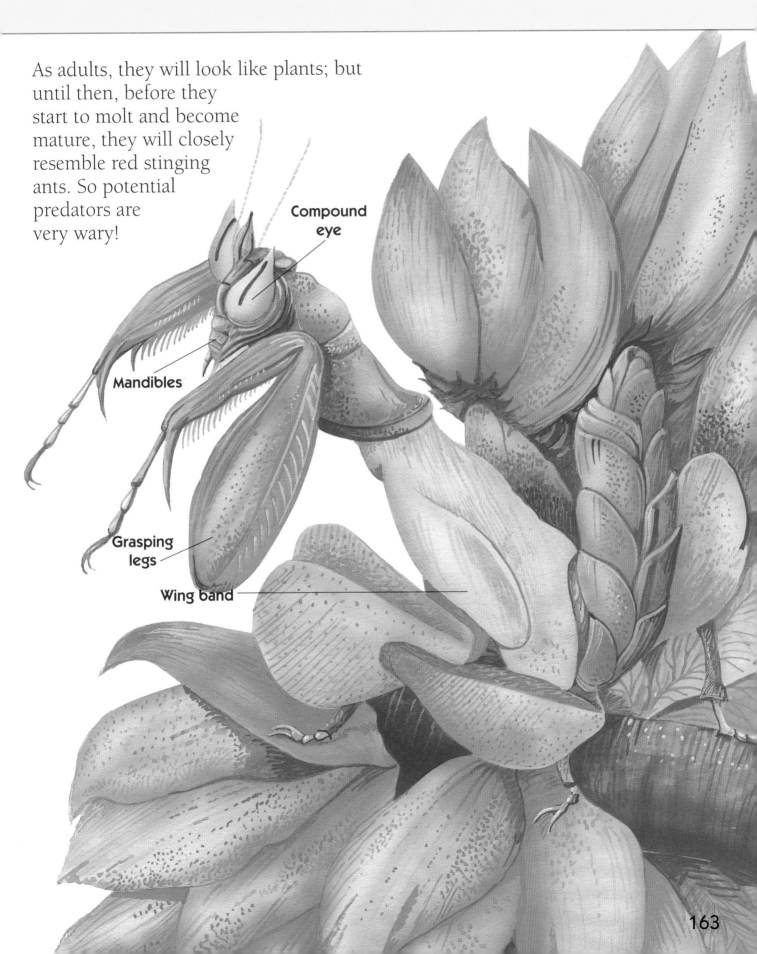

Compound eye

Mandibles

Grasping legs

Wing band

Crickets

True crickets make astonishingly loud music. The males rub their wings together and produce a high-pitched sound, using a different sort of mechanism from the one used by the grasshopper.

There are several types of true crickets. Most look very much like grasshoppers, but there are, in fact, distinct differences to look for. You might like to turn back to pages 82-83 at this point. True crickets are broader and flatter in appearance, and their wings and wing-cases also lie flat.

True crickets produce their song in a slightly different way from the grasshoppers, too. They have a file-like ridge on their wing covers. They open and close the wing-covers just partially; and as they do so, the file of one is drawn over the scraper on the other. (Both wings have a file *and* a scraper.) The resulting vibrating sound is then amplified by what is called a drum-head, lying just behind the file-ridge. Like grasshoppers, though, crickets have their hearing organs in their legs.

Most true crickets live outdoors, but one of the best-known species has taken to the indoor life. Inside our homes it is warm and safe. This house-cricket has a particularly loud song, and claims have been made that it may be heard as far as one mile (1.6km) away! What is more, their presence in

World of the cricket

- Many crickets, if disturbed, can throw their voices, just like ventriloquists. The sound seems to be coming from elsewhere, and this completely confuses any predators.

a home is thought to be a very lucky omen by those who are superstitious.

Sing though they do, and sounding happy enough, male crickets sometimes become very aggressive in the mating season, and fights may even break out between rivals for the females' favors, as you can see *opposite*.

In some parts of the world, a few people even keep male field crickets as caged pets. They provide entertainment by singing and also by fighting. They would doubtless be much happier in the wild.

FACTFILE

Members of the cricket family include the wood-cricket, the mole-cricket, and the wingless scaly cricket, all slightly different.

Stick insects

Next time you are at a zoo with an insect house, it would be worthwhile taking a look at any stick insects that they have – surely among the most interesting of creepy-crawlies to grace our planet.

Some stick insects are aptly named because, quite simply, they look just like long, thin sticks. This is actually the secret of their success. Stick insects look so much like sticks, leaves, or twigs that they are often entirely overlooked by predators. Not only do their bodies look like some sort of vegetation, but their legs can be also held at an angle so that their limbs closely resemble side-shoots on a plant stalk.

Let's now take a look at the structure of a stick insect's body. At the top of the head are two long antennae, used for feeling the way ahead. The mouth, meanwhile, has surprisingly strong jaws for such a frail-looking creature, which are used for chewing on plants.

The stick insect's six legs (and wings, in some types) are attached to the thorax, behind which is the stick insect's abdomen.

At the end of the feet are tiny claws. These help the insect grip a twig or to hold on to a moving branch. Stick insects can even use them to walk upside down along a leaf or twig without falling.

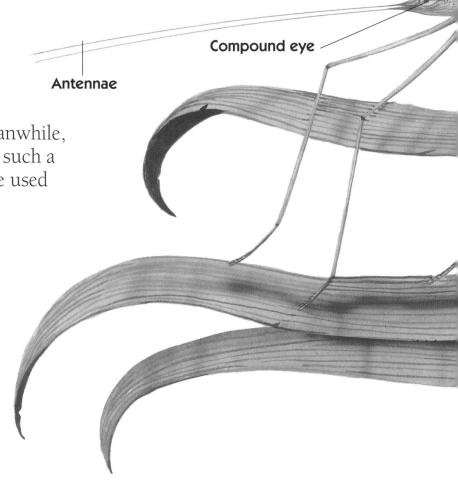

Antennae

Compound eye

FACTFILE

The female stick insect will lay several eggs in a single day, and it will be many months before they start to hatch.

166

World of the stick insect

- Not only are adult leaf and stick insects expertly camouflaged, even their eggs closely resemble plant seeds, making their survival more likely.

Their legs are not made for grabbing their next meal, like the front legs of a praying mantis, either. But, then, stick insects rarely need to move quickly. There are two reasons for this.

Wing case and wings

Abdomen

Thorax

Stick insects do not have the mobility of some of their fellows in the insect kingdom, however. Their legs are not designed for jumping, like a grasshopper's for instance.

In the vegetation around them, they are almost invisible to most predators. And because they are strictly herbivores, they do not ever need to chase after other creatures for a meal.

Masters of disguise

There are about 2,000 different types of stick and leaf insects in the world, but you will always have to look very carefully to find them.

Stick insects are such superb masters of disguise that they often look just like the vegetation surrounding them, as you can see from the two very different types illustrated *below* and on the opposite page. They have this ability to camouflage themselves right from the time that they are born.

When one hatches on the ground, the emerging stick insect may be brown to match the fallen twigs and leaves around it. Later, once some climb up to fresh leaves, they have the ability to change to a shade of green. Other stick insects, however, may be mottled and so will be very well hidden on tree bark.

Even if they move from time to time, perhaps swaying from side to side, they will probably look just like thin twigs or leaves blowing in the breeze. However, the wings of stick insects can sometimes be quite colorful, if they have wings. The color will remain hidden, though, and only show when the wings are unfolded, which happens if the stick insects are disturbed. Scientists call this process "flash coloration", and stick insects find it useful for frightening off any would-be predators.

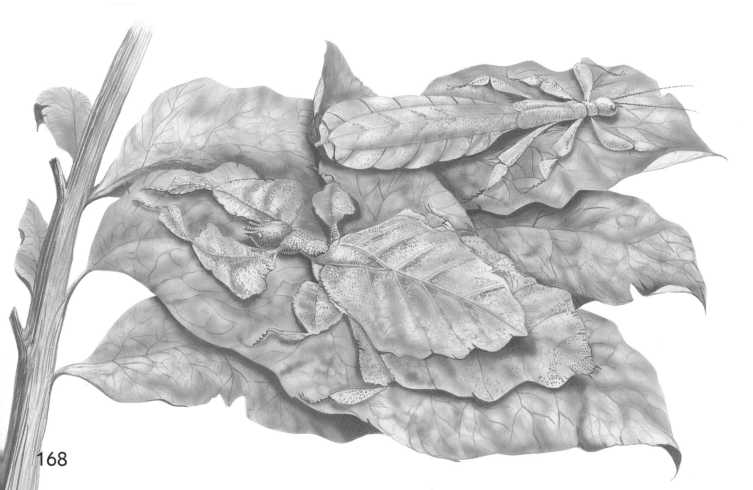

World of the stick insect

- Stick insects belong to a group called *Phasmida*, meaning "ghost". What a good name for insects that are hard to spot!

- Bats, other small mammals, birds, and lizards are the principal predators likely to make a ready meal of stick insects when, of course, they can find them.

You will need to examine vegetation carefully to spot a stick insect. And remember, some can even change color in the course of a single day.

Most walking stick insects are silent; and even when they eat, they do so very quietly. This, of course, helps keep them camouflaged.

However, one type of the stick insect – the jungle nymph, which inhabits the thick, impenetrable rain forests of Malaysia – makes a strong hissing sound if it is about to be attacked. This, combined with the hundreds of needle-sharp prickles on its body, soon scares off would-be predators.

169

Creatures of the night

Just when you are about to go to bed each evening, stick insects begin to stir themselves, preparing to munch on their breakfast. Holes left in vegetation, as shown in this illustration, are a sign that they have had their fill of plants. But they are always vulnerable to predators.

Stick insects wake up in the evening, preferring to get plenty of rest by day and then feeding after sunset.

During the day, they remain entirely motionless, hiding among twigs or bark. Even if they are knocked off their branch – blown off by the wind, perhaps – and drop to the ground, they will lie still wherever they land, refusing to draw attention to themselves.

But when darkness falls, stick insects are ready to go looking for a feast. They do not usually travel far for their meals, however, and may even live on the very same plant that will form the main item in their diet for their entire lives.

Once they are moving, stick insects are no longer so well camouflaged and therefore more vulnerable to attack. But, under cover of darkness, they are, of course, less likely to be noticed by one of their many predators in the animal world.

If a stick insect is attacked when it is young and loses a leg, it will usually manage to grow back a replacement for the severed limb, so that it can soon walk normally again.

FACTFILE

The longest stick insect discovered so far is the giant stick insect from Indonesia, which grows to all of 12in (30cm) in length.

Unusual pets

Insects are not often kept as pets. Some are very difficult to look after, while others are thought to be too unattractive. But stick insects are different and are, in fact, the most popular insects to keep at home.

If you would like to keep stick insects, you should be able to buy some from a pet shop or specialist breeder. Most come from the tropical regions of Central and South America, Australia, Asia, and Africa. Only a few species are ever to be found wild in Europe and North America.

It would be best to purchase them at the nymph stage, but after they have had several molts. Check that they have all six legs and that their bodies look healthy. Take advice, too, about caring for them from the person who sells you your new pets. You can take them home in a box with air holes in the lid and with some suitable plants inside for them to feed on. However, eventually, you will need a permanent "house" for your stick insects.

World of the stick insect

- Male stick insects with wings generally have bigger wings than the females, which are usually plumper.

This "house" could be an aquarium with a special top to provide good ventilation. Make sure they have plenty of space. If they are overcrowded, they will not be able to feed properly and may start to fight.

Blackberry leaves will provide an ideal diet for most stick insects, and some will eat privet or rhododendron leaves.

Keep these moist with a plant spray. Be sure to put twigs in the tank, too. Your stick insects need to have something to climb on. Some types of stick insects like to drink as well, so you will need to give them fresh water regularly, in a shallow dish.

The paper floor covering will need to be changed a couple of times each week to keep the tank hygienic. Look after your stick insects well, and they should live their full life span of anything from one month to a year. If you are lucky, they might even lay eggs and provide you with a new generation of stick insects.

Some stick insects are parthenogenetic, which means that the males play no part at all in the birth of the young.

CAREFUL HANDLING

Remember to handle your stick insects very delicately. Larger ones can be picked up if you hold them gently on both sides of the thorax. You will need to move them very gently when you take them from a plant to avoid damaging their legs. Some, such as the jungle nymph, have sharp spines and powerful legs, and will draw blood if handled roughly. A few species also have glands that emit a nasty-smelling liquid. If this comes into contact with your eyes, it may cause painful swelling and even temporary blindness.

Earwigs

Look under a log, a pile of leaves, or on a plant, and you may find one or two earwigs, or even a dozen.

Earwigs generally hide during the day, coming out only at night to forage for food. Almost anything will satisfy their appetites – fruit, flowers, rotting vegetation, or small insects, for instance. You may sometimes be lucky enough to spot them during the day, though.

HEARSAY

About as long as your top thumb joint, and brownish in color, earwigs got their name because people once thought they liked running into human ears in order to bite through the eardrum.

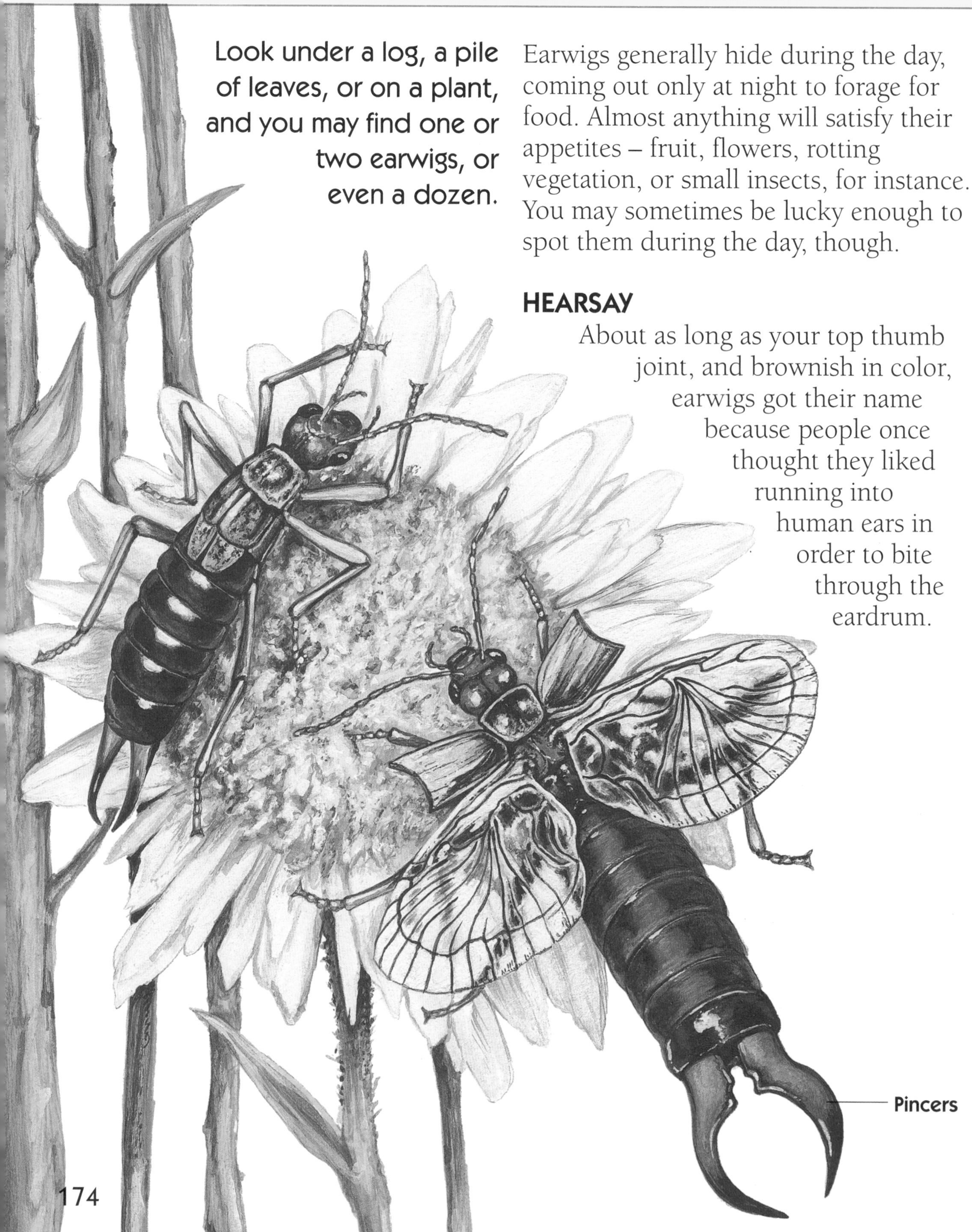

Pincers

174

No one today believes this – even if, just once in a while, an earwig accidentally enters the ear of someone sleeping outdoors. It is interesting, too, to note that the earwig's wings, when folded, can look like a human ear, so this might be another reason for the name.

If it is disturbed or attacked, an earwig will immediately arch the pincers at the back of its body in a reflex action and bring these forward over the top of its body in scorpion-like fashion. The earwig also uses its pincers to catch other insects for food. In the male, the pincers are much larger and also curved. You should therefore be able to identify which is the male and which is the female in the illustration on the opposite page.

One of the two earwigs, as you can see, has its wings exposed. They are large, yet delicate, and usually kept folded away under its tegmina, or wing cases. The process of such folding is highly elaborate – once they are folded in place, there will be about 40 layers. (Find a piece of paper the size of one page of this book, try to fold it forty times, and you will soon realize how complicated this is.) Among the one thousand or so species of earwigs, however, some

World of the earwig

- Earwigs are harmless creatures but may annoy gardeners, because they enjoy munching on petals so much.

- The wings of earwigs are almost semi-circular and exceedingly thin. In fact, the name of the order of insects to which they belong – *Dermaptera* – means "skin-winged."

no longer have wings, while others do not ever use them, possibly because of the complexity of folding them back.

FAMILY BONDS

Unusual for insects, earwigs are exceptionally good parents. Male and female earwigs bond and are loyal to each other after mating, which usually takes place in late summer. The small white eggs will then hatch in early spring. The female will even retrieve eggs that have become scattered. She will also attack any predator, and constantly cleans the eggs to prevent them from developing mold. The nymphs are fed by the mother, and she continues to do so even when they are near to reaching maturity.

FACTFILE

Most types of earwigs usually lay between 20 and 40 eggs at one time, but it can be as many as 80 in some species.

Termites

A single termite mound can house as many as five million of these extraordinary insects. They are useful in that they clear up dead wood, but can also completely ruin buildings with their voracious appetites.

Termites are light-colored insects from tropical parts of the world, such as Africa and South America. Their way of life is a lot like that of ants – so similar, in fact, that they are sometimes called "white ants." But, in fact, they are not closely related. Interestingly, the closest relative to a termite is the cockroach! They look very different from ants, too – their bodies are softer and paler than ants' bodies, and they do not have the narrow waist ants have.

MASTER NEST-BUILDERS

Termites usually live underground. Some grow fungi, like some ants, and others collect grain, like harvester ants, for food. But they eat dead wood, too, which ants rarely do. Unlike ants, some termites also build tall nests called mounds, using soil and wood, as well as their own droppings and saliva. Some of these nests have amazing shapes like the one you can see here, and may even reach a height of more than 18ft (5m), which is three times the size of a tall adult human being.

EGG-LAYING MACHINE

Like an ants' nest, a termite colony starts with a male and a queen mating in a swarm. But unlike ants, the male – or king – does not die but stays with the queen in the nest. There may even be more than one king.

The queen lays up to 30,000 eggs every day, and her body gets terribly distorted in the process. She becomes, in fact, like a giant egg-laying machine. Blind worker termites of either sex look after the nest and there are blind soldiers, too, to defend it, as with ants. The female worker and soldier termites never fly, nor do they normally lay eggs, as the queens do.

The young termites are known as nymphs; and when they are ready to hatch from their eggs, they already look like adult termites and immediately start feeding on regurgitated wood.

Although they clear up dead wood, termites are usually regarded as pests because of the terrible damage they can do to buildings by eating away at them.

World of the termite

- Some termite soldiers spray poison in the form of a sticky substance if attacked, and may even explode while they are spraying.

Lice

Tiny and flat, with claws, lice spend their whole lives on a host, and can easily pass from one host to another, feeding on blood and skin.

Greatly magnified, the louse (*plural*, lice) that you can see here is climbing up a human hair and will soon be ready to feed on the poor victim's scalp. It is actually so small that it is barely visible to the human eye. But just look at those nasty claws! It will hold on to the skin with its proboscis, and then pierce with the three stylets of its mouth-parts, causing intense irritation. It may even lay its eggs, known as nits, in the hair.

The nits look like yellow lumps and may be present around the ears and near the hairline. There may be as many as 50-100 laid at one time, and they soon hatch. Three weeks later, some of them, too, will be ready to lay their own batch of nits. They love the temperature of the human body.

NO DISGRACE

The possible transfer of lice from one person to another is a prime reason for not sharing brushes or combs, and for keeping your hair regularly washed.

It is an alarming thought that such horrid little bugs could get on to your scalp; but if you ever get lice, it may not be your fault. Children who huddle close together – perhaps sharing a book during a lesson at school – may be vulnerable. The lice have strong claws, enabling them to withstand all but the most vigorous scratching. But a doctor or pharmacist should be able to recommend a special lotion to help get rid of them.

Lice may also be present in dirty clothes. In fact, whenever people gather closely together – perhaps after a natural disaster where they are unable to keep clean – lice can be a problem.

World of the lice

- Some species of lice will pass on certain diseases to livestock and so must be very carefully controlled to avoid an epidemic among the herd or flock.

FACTFILE

One type of lice will infest the pubic region of adult humans only, if there is poor hygiene resulting from infrequent washing.

They may even spread the dangerous disease, typhus, characterized by a high fever, rash, and severe headache. This disease was once a great threat to armies because of the poor conditions in which soldiers had to live when a war was on. Vaccines, however, have been developed against typhus, and conditions have generally improved, even in battle regions.

What is particularly strange is that some lice are so exactly adapted to living on their hosts that they could not cope with attaching themselves to the hair of another type of host which may have a different thickness. (There are even two sorts of human louse, one infesting the hair and the other, the body.)

SUCKERS AND BITERS

Some lice bite, while others suck. The biting kind are mainly associated with birds, while the suckers are parasites of mammals, including humans. The sight of both types is poor and, with evolution, they have lost their wings; yet they seem to have no trouble in finding refuge on a host.

Most biting lice are under 0.2in (6mm) long, with hard, flat bodies and fairly large heads. As insects, they each have six legs and each one ends in one or two claws – appendages that enable them to cling on tightly to their reluctant hosts, on to whose hair or feathers they will stick their many eggs. The human body, however, does not provide a suitable environment for biting lice. It is just as well: sucking lice are quite enough to cope with!

In all, there are well over 2,500 different known species of these miniature bloodsuckers and biters; and, so far, scientists have not succeeded in eradicating them. We can only keep ourselves as clean as possible to cut down their numbers.

Weevils

There are thought to be tens of thousands of different weevils, highly destructive members of the even larger beetle family.

Some weevils are so minute that you can barely see them at all with the naked eye. Others are larger, but even the giant species from tropical regions of the world rarely exceed 3in (7.5cm) in length.

Weevils, such as the boll weevil, *left*, and the wire weevil on a leaf, *far right*, feed exclusively on plant material. In fact, most weevils are exceedingly particular about their diet and will only feed on certain types of plants. Thus, the pine weevil feeds on forest pines, the palm weevil feeds on coconut palms; the apple blossom weevil feeds on apple blossom; and the cotton boll weevil feeds on cotton plants. And what a menace the cotton boll weevil has proved itself to be! The female may lay around 200 eggs at a time, one in each bud; and the larvae proceed to develop there, causing complete devastation to a plantation very quickly.

Infestation by weevils can thus bring farmers enormous problems, both practical and economical. But, ironically, in a few instances, the voracious appetites of these insects have

World of the weevil

● Some male weevils will fight with rivals over females; and some types are so chivalrous they stand by the females until they lay their eggs.

● If you find a bad hazelnut, it may once have been home to a tiny weevil grub that fed on the kernel before gnawing its way out.

been put to advantage. A weevil that feeds exclusively on water ferns, for example, was intentionally introduced into an Australian reservoir from which thousands of tons of water ferns had to be cleared. Within one year, entirely on their own, the weevils had carried out this formidable task, without any need for dredgers or human effort.

MIXED CROPS

In the past, farmers in the southern United States have actually expressed gratitude to the cotton boll weevil for the way in which it forced them to farm additional crops and

thereby reap greater financial rewards. Every year, dedicated entomologists worldwide find a few hundred new species of weevil; so there may be many more of these tiny insects waiting to be discovered, especially in the tropical rainforests.

FACTFILE

Strange but true – some types of grain weevils are much smaller than the grains of the type of cereal they like to eat.

Aphids

Outright enemies of gardeners and farmers, aphids can infest in immense numbers. Not only do they suck plants dry of their sap, they can also spread plant diseases.

If you ever see a magnificent plant, such as a rose bush, that is covered with tiny greenflies – a type of aphid – do not imagine that they are just lying there, asleep or sunbathing. Far from it; each and every one of the hundreds of these little monsters is likely to be feeding by plunging its snout into the plant's sap and severely damaging the leaves and stems in this way. Even worse, they leave the plant exposed to harmful bacterial infection.

There can be no doubt at all that aphids are plant-destroyers and therefore not welcome in field or garden. Ladybugs, like the one in this illustration, though, love them and will consume great quantities of these tiny creatures. Farmers may even opt to introduce certain ladybugs as a natural form of aphid control.

Ladybugs. and their larvae, then, are among aphids' main enemies. Others include spiders, hover flies and lacewings. But some types of aphids can exude a waxy substance that will paralyze a predator. A number also seem to taste disgusting to predators; others secrete a chemical that will halt the development of any parasitic insect larvae that may try to feed on them.

SUGARY SECRETIONS

Ants, meanwhile, love the much more pleasant sugary secretions of aphids, known as honeydew. This is secreted through the aphids' anus, and ants crave the substance so much that, in order to get at it, they will tend the aphids, protect them from predators, and even herd them together. If ants did not milk aphids in this way, the secreted honeydew would smother the plant and probably kill it. Gardeners, therefore, are grateful, on the one hand, to ants for saving their plants from suffocation; but, on the other hand, they certainly do not appreciate the increased aphid

World of the aphid

- Aphids reproduce in fascinating ways. Sometimes there are only females in the aphid population, and these will reproduce other females only, without mating – that is, parthenogenetically. When their offspring in turn reproduce, there will be males and females, which then mate and produce daughters only.

population, due to the ants' taste for honeydew and the care they take of the aphids. Ants will even welcome aphids into their nests and allow them to lay their eggs there.

Some aphids can feed on any type of plant, but other species stick to one type. Breeding at an extraordinary rate; groups of the winged females may leave one plant and waft to another, sometimes over considerable distances, so that areas once free of them may unexpectedly become infested.

FACTFILE

Aphids breed very quickly. Even before they are born, in fact, they have young aphids developing inside them.

Spiders

Some spiders are so small, they can fit on a pinhead; others can cover your dinner plate. Some are skinny; others are far fatter and even furry. But all spiders have a remarkably similar body structure.

Some people squeal when they see a spider in the bathtub or crawling up a wall. But there is no need to be frightened. Most spiders just want to get away to weave a web and catch a tasty insect, not a human!

The house spider is, in fact, just one of some 40,000 species of spiders that are found all over the world, except at the polar regions. In fact, spiders have been around on Planet Earth a long time, too – over 300 million years, so experts think.

Male and female spiders' bodies have two main parts, as you can see here – the head and chest (thorax), and also the abdomen. But the female's abdomen is bigger than the male's. This is so she can produce large numbers of eggs.

Abdomen

Leg

FACTFILE

If, by accident, you step on a spider and squash it, you will not find a red mess. This is because its blood is pale blue or green.

A spider cannot fly, so it has no wings. But its eight long legs make it a champion runner and a very good climber. Using special tufts of hair that allow them to grip smooth surfaces,

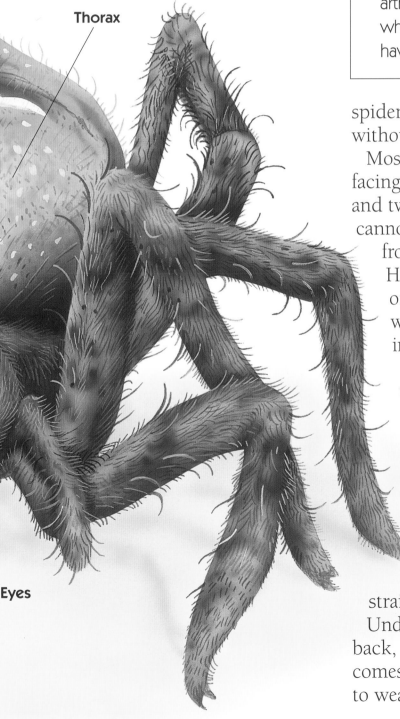

Thorax

Eyes

World of the spider

- Spiders are part of a group of arthropods known as *Arachnids*, to which scorpions also belong. They have existed for over 400 million years.

spiders can even walk on ceilings without falling off.

Most spiders have eight eyes – two facing forwards, four looking upwards, and two guarding the rear – so you cannot be sure to creep up on a spider from behind without being noticed! However, the many-eyed spider is often short-sighted. Still, it can tell where it is – and if there is an insect about – by using its feelers.

These feelers, or palps, look like two short legs at the front of its body. It can even smell with them. Now look between the palps. Can you see two wicked-looking parts? These are the spider's jaws which can crush a captured insect and poison it to death. The spider then sucks the liquid centre of its meal straight into its mouth, very greedily. Under a spider's abdomen at the very back, are its spinnerets. The spider's silk comes out of these organs, and is used to weave its webs.

Building a home

Spiders are amazingly skilled spinners and will quickly build the most beautiful webs as traps for the prey on which they feed. Once caught, victims will rarely escape.

When the Scottish king, Robert the Bruce, took shelter in a cave on the eve of the battle of Bannockburn, way back in 1314, he happened to see a spider trying to weave a web across the mouth of the cave, but failing. The spider kept on trying, though, until at last it succeeded. Its courage inspired the great king to do exactly the same in battle the next day – and he won!

Many spiders spin large, circular webs, known as orb-webs, to catch

flying insects, just like the one being woven across these two pages.

You have probably seen orb-webs in gardens, among the trees and bushes, or in the house, between ceilings and light fixtures. They seem to appear by magic, as if from nowhere; but this is not in fact the case because, for the spider, they involve a lot of intricate work.

A FRAME-UP

So how does the spider begin its web? First, it chooses a point that will be the top of the web and spins a single thread. The spider then waits for a breeze to waft it to the next anchor point. It now continues to be wafted in this way from place to place, spinning as it goes, until it has a basic frame for the web.

The spider next weaves spokes from the frame to a central point. Then, it spins silk around and around the spokes in ever-increasing circles, until

FACTFILE

Orb-web spiders can spin webs with about one thousand connections in less than an hour, using 100yds (92m) of silk.

temporary spiral. Time, now, for a rest, as the spider waits for its next meal to fly into the trap. Spiders also use their silk to tie up any victims, such as flies, that get caught in the web.

But not all webs are like this. The purse-web spider, for instance, lives in a silken tube, most of which is underground. The part above ground looks like the finger of a glove. The spider hides inside and drags passing insects through the walls of the web. Other spiders spin webs like funnels, which also lead to an underground lair. Here, they lurk in ambush, waiting to pounce on any insects that happen to step on the web.

the pattern is at last complete. All this time, the spider has been using a temporary spiral as a platform from which to operate. When the web is complete, the spider will then eat the

Disappearing tricks

Some spiders conceal themselves from prey by resembling other things – bird droppings, for instance. Others may change color.

Take a look at the picture on the lefthand page. How many spiders can you see? One or two, perhaps. But look again, and you will probably be able to spot quite a few that are not immediately visible.

Spiders need to blend in with their surroundings, so that they do not scare away their next meal, and also to protect themselves from enemies. Many are a simple, dull brown or black. This is just right for scuttling along the ground. But even those with stripes or patches of different colors may be well camouflaged and difficult to see against particular backgrounds.

The black-and-white striped zebra spider, for example, lives on stone walls and buildings, where it almost disappears into its surroundings.

Other types of spiders have a knobby texture on their bodies that merges perfectly with the bark of trees. There are even spiders – the amazing crab

spiders, for instance – that can actually change their color to suit the circumstances! They do not need to spin a web to catch prey, but simply wait for some juicy-looking unsuspecting insects to pass by. If a yellow flower seems the best hide-out, for example – as in the illustration *below* – the crab spider can automatically turn yellow to blend in with the petals. Then, when an insect comes up close, the "invisible" crab spider pounces – and dinner is ready!

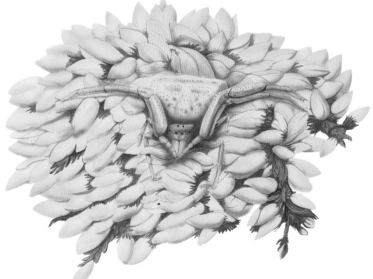

Attracting a mate

Any courting male spider has to be very careful in the mating process. The female is not readily responsive, and may think he is a meal!

Imagine that you are a male Mexican lynx spider, and the attractive female, *below*, sitting not very far away from you, is twice your size, maybe even bigger, and would rather dine on you than make friends. What do you do? Well, you will have to be extremely brave, and use a range of tricks to persuade her to like you long enough to mate. What are these wily ways, then?

Well, strange as it may seem, you can dance, make music, or give presents – just like humans do when they are courting! First, you find the female by following her scent. Next, you wriggle your body and stamp your feet in the hope that she will be so impressed with your dazzling dance display that she allows you to come nearer. Or, you might carefully step on to the edge of her web and pluck out a special rhythm on its strands, just as a human musician does when strumming a tune on a guitar. This special musical message will inform her that you are not a meal.

FACTFILE

Some male jumping spiders have bright splashes of color on their palps, which are displayed in their mating dance.

You might, however, prefer to catch an insect and wrap it up in your own silk. The female, you hope, will be so interested in your present to her that she will allow you to come close without attacking you. She may even respond by waving her legs and palps around in the air and by moving towards you as you approach her.

After mating, however, you could be in great danger from your mate. In spite of all your efforts to woo her, you will still look like a meal to her! The black widow spider is known sometimes to eat her mate, and many other species, including yours, would perhaps do the same if given the chance.

ENTICING SCENT

Many female spiders actually give off a special scent with their silk. The scent helps a male spider identify the female as one of his own species, and therefore assists him in getting down to his courting behavior right away. (He will not mate with a female of another species). The scent does not linger for long; but at least this means that he does not waste time if his potential mate has already scuttled off.

World of the spider

- Some male spiders mate with several females, but it weakens them and they may end up being eaten by one, having no energy left to escape.

The black widow's bite

Most spiders use venom to kill or paralyze their prey before devouring it. But a few can also be very poisonous to humans.

It is a dramatic scene. An enormous, ugly-looking spider sinks its fangs into someone's skin. The pain is awful, and the victim begins to sweat, feeling very ill. But then a doctor arrives with an antidote, and saves him from serious illness, or even death.

Luckily, there are not many spiders with venom as strong as this, and they do not attack first. So it is unlikely you will ever be bitten by one of these spiders in ordinary daily life. But you cannot rely on a doctor being there if you are bitten, so you will need to take care if ever you are anywhere near these deadly types.

FANGED MINI-BEASTS

All spiders have fangs, or jaws, which they use to bite their prey. Never annoy a spider, because a few species may bite to protect themselves from you, and that could be quite painful or, in some cases, even fatal.

One spider that has been accused unjustly of being a killer, however, is the tarantula. This is probably because of its fearsome-sounding name. The very word conjures up a repulsive, furry monster that is waiting to strike with its deadly poison.

Well, it *is* large and furry, but its bite is about as dangerous as the sting from a bee, and so it is usually quite harmless to most humans.

The real terror is the Black Widow spider, shown in the illustration *opposite*. It has this name because the female sometimes feasts on the male after mating. It is small – only 0.6in (15mm) long – but its venom is lethal and much more poisonous than that of a rattlesnake, for example.

The pain will start about 15 minutes after it has bitten you, at first in the groin area, and then spreading to the abdomen and elsewhere. Breathing may become difficult, too.

So keep away from black widows! You can sometimes recognize them because many have a distinctive red hourglass-shaped mark on their abdomen.

FACTFILE

Other spiders with poisonous bites include the Brown Recluse spider, and the Wandering spider from tropical America.

True bugs

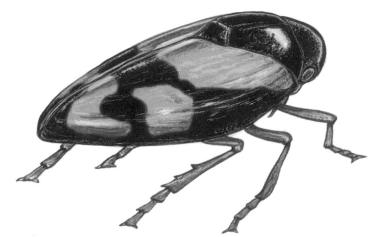

This large family of insects includes about 50,000 species. Several are featured elsewhere in this book. On these two pages, we introduce a few more fascinating examples of true bugs.

The word *bug* is generally used to refer to any sort of small creepy-crawly that does not have a backbone. Strictly, however, the word *bug* refers to a number of insects that have piercing mouthparts held under their bodies when not in use.

Most also have two pairs of wings, as well as antennae; but the many species vary a great deal in appearance. What is more, not all are carnivorous. In fact, most simply suck at plants, causing harm to vegetation.

The scientific term for true bugs is *Hemiptera*. The aphids, cicadas, assassin bugs, bed bugs and water bugs belong to this group.

The frog hopper, *top left*, is another true bug. It is cute enough to look at, but can do a lot of harm in the garden. The young produce a substance known as cuckoo spit, which you may have seen on plants. It is frothy and provides protection so that they are hidden from predators that might otherwise like a meal of them.

The froth is called cuckoo spit because it usually occurs at about the same time of year as the first cuckoo.

If you now look at the illustration shown *bottom left*, you will see a female stink bug with her eggs. Fortunately, it is only a drawing and you do not

need to hold your nose! Live ones produce a highly offensive odor if disturbed in any way, to ward off predators. They are also known as shieldbugs, and the mothers make very good parents, waiting close by until the eggs hatch. They also stay with the young until they can fend for themselves. Brightly colored, their bodies warn predators of their foul taste; as soon as they meet with an enemy, they will emit the bad-smelling liquid.

NOT JUST A KISS

Some bugs also spread disease. The kissing bug is an example and is shown on this page. It is a type of assassin bug and native to Central and South America. Beware of it, if you are in these regions. And how did it get its name? Well, it likes to bite human faces, and can sometimes spread Chagas disease through its feces. This is a disease with symptoms of fever and heart damage. Some bugs may look endearing; but as you now know, many of them can cause considerable damage.

Near the water

Every stagnant pond, every rippling stream, every winding river, and every wide ocean is home to all sorts of bugs that enjoy living in or near the water.

Next time you are in a waterside environment, whether beside the sea, a lake, or a canal – be sure to watch out for bugs. You might find some interesting larvae, too, as some land bugs spend the early part of their lives in water, only graduating to the ground or to the air when fully mature.

You might be lucky enough to spot a whirligig beetle, for example. You will know it at once because it spins round and round in a circle, almost non-stop, so that you are bound to get the impression that it ends up feeling terribly dizzy. It dives occasionally, too, but comes up for air.

Some water bugs, however, can take in a supply of oxygen directly from the water. Others are able to carry bubbles of air on their tails, their chests, or their backs. A number, though, prefer to pass the time resting on their backs on the surface.

Pond-skaters, meanwhile, closely resemble stick insects. The more fearsome carnivorous species of water-beetles may well go hunting for them. Water-scorpions are greedy predators, too. They may seem to have only two pairs of legs, but in fact there are three. The third is used as claws – perfectly-formed instruments for seizing any unsuspecting creature that happens to cross their path.

Such creatures are wily. Dragonflies, however, are perhaps the most beautiful of all waterside bugs, as you will discover as you read the fact-packed pages that follow.

Dragonflies

A few species of dragonflies have become extinct in recent years, but over 5,000 different types remain in many parts of the world.

The most obvious things about a dragonfly are its beautiful wings. It has two pairs, with a dark mark on the tip of each. They are very thin and gauze-like, with a pattern of fine veins that help keep them stiff. Even when resting, dragonflies have their magnificent wings outspread.

Different sorts of dragonflies have different patterns on their wings. Many also have bright blue or green bodies, but some are red or orange; a few are decorated with black and yellow stripes.

A dragonfly has a fairly large head for an insect of its size, and can turn it around in almost all directions. At the front are two big eyes, and there are three small ones at the top of its head.

Below the eyes are jaws with saw-like teeth, which the dragonfly finds useful for biting its prey.

A dragonfly's two tiny antennae, for touching and smelling, are also on its head, but are not always visible because they can be finer than a human hair.

A dragonfly's long, thin body has two main parts. The first, the thorax, houses its strong wing muscles. Its six legs, joined to this part of its body, are thin and covered with bristles. The dragonfly uses them to cling on to a plant when resting. They are not much use for walking, but do help with catching prey.

FACTFILE

The smallest dragonfly known lives in Burma. It has a wingspan and body each only as big as your middle fingernail.

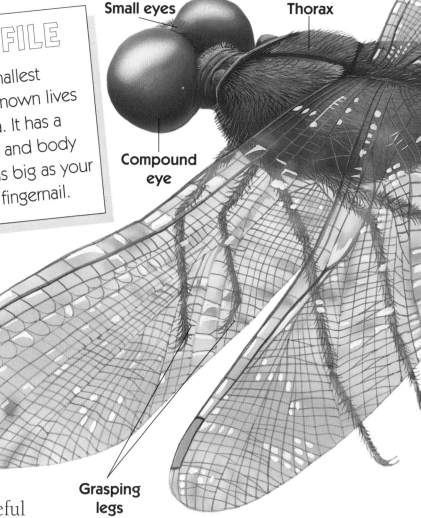

Small eyes

Thorax

Compound eye

Grasping legs

on a reed, by the time you count up to twenty, the chances are that it will probably have taken to the air again, hovering, diving, or swerving this way and that.

Dragonflies also have the ability to fly for surprisingly long distances, and they can fly backward just as easily. Many may even reach extraordinary speeds – up to 65mph (104km/h) over short distances in some cases. At their fastest, a dragonfly's wings will beat at up to 30 times a second – so fast it is almost impossible for us to see them move, and they can even turn somersaults in the air. In fact, it is their flying speed and acrobatics that help dragonflies escape most predators that would like a meal of them.

Abdomen

Clasper

The second part of a dragonfly's body is its abdomen. Inside are its stomach and breathing equipment. It has no lungs but has thin tubes that take in air and carry it around the body. At the end of its abdomen there are two pincers, or claspers, which a male dragonfly uses to hold on to a female when mating.

During daylight hours, you will hardly ever see a dragonfly sitting still for more than a few seconds. If you do spot one

World of the dragonfly

- Dragonflies live in all parts of the world where there is water, warm weather, and plenty of food.

- Dragonflies are known to have existed way back in prehistoric times, when some species were exceptionally large.

Birth of a dragonfly

The development of a dragonfly from nymph stage to its full adult form involves an almost magical metamorphosis.

An adult dragonfly may live for only about two weeks. Even the longest-living die after about six weeks. But this is only one stage of its life.

When a male dragonfly is ready to mate, it will wander around a watery place for a week or so. During this time, it will be marking off some territory as its own and driving away any rival males.

Then it will be ready to select a female. First, it tries to grab her head or body with its legs. If the female is willing, they then fly off together, and the male mates with her. The two then part, and the female soon lays her yellow eggs on water weeds, in mud or in water. Different types of dragonflies lay their eggs in different places.

The eggs usually hatch between two and five weeks later. When the larva, or nymph, eventually comes out of the egg, it lives under the water at first. The wingless nymph can breathe here through the use of special organs, known as gills. For the next two years, it will hunt other insects, and even fish at times.

200

During its nymph stage – which is much longer than its adult life – it will shed its skin as many as 15 times.

BREAKING FREE

When the nymph is fully grown, it will instinctively crawl up a plant from the water into the air, and hang there. Amazingly, the nymph's skin now gradually splits, so its head and body can break free. The creature that emerges is a fully grown dragonfly.

World of the dragonfly

- Dragonflies have very large, colorful, bulging eyes. These have 30,000 different six-sided parts, which enable them to see almost all around them, and to spot a likely meal that is moving up to 39ft (12m) away.

One of the names that dragonflies are also known by is, strangely, "horse-stinger," but these insects have no sting at all and are harmless to humans.

In fact, they do a lot of good by keeping down the mosquito and fly population – insect pests that make up the greater part of their diet.

DRAGONFLIES
Water-lovers

Exquisitely beautiful, dragonflies are among the swiftest of insects. So where are you likely to find them?

The best place to spot dragonflies is near water. Although some dragonflies fly in summer through open woodlands and rest in the sun on bushes, they all have to visit watery places to mate. The females will then lay their eggs in water.

A large pond with clean water may sometimes be a home for as many as six different species of dragonflies. Some skim low through the reeds, while others patrol backward and forward, above open water.

However, some dragonflies seem to prefer boggy pools where the water is dark and acid. Others are found by fast-flowing mountain streams, stagnant ponds, broad rivers, canals or still lakes.

No one knows why dragonflies choose to live near one body of water rather than another. But when a dragonfly visits water for the first time, it often dips in its abdomen. This may be to check that it is not just a puddle that might dry up in the sun. Whichever type of watery place a dragonfly selects, it likes one with some pond weed and reeds or other plants growing along the banks. It can use these as resting

World of the dragonfly

- Dragonflies are divided into two types – darters and hawkers. Darters, true to their name, dart from their perches to catch food or chase away rivals. Hawkers, meanwhile, will patrol up and down a stretch of water on the look-out for a likely meal.

perches, and nymphs will automatically crawl up them immediately after they emerge from under the water, ready to turn into adult dragonflies.

DRAGONFLY LEGENDS

There are many popular legends associated with the dragonfly that originate from all over the world. In Japan, for instance, these graceful creatures were once thought to be very lucky, and symbolic of courage. In Great Britain, it was a very widespread belief that the appearance of dragonflies would lead good boys to places where they were sure to catch lots of fish. Meanwhile, in North America, it was once thought that if someone was foolish enough to kill a dragonfly, then a member of his or her family was destined to die, too.

Hide-and-seek

Often described as the queens of all the water insects, dragonflies love sunny days and will hide from us when it is cloudy.

When the weather is fine, you may be lucky enough to spot a few of these gloriously graceful creatures, with their characteristic bulging eyes and glistening wings. Even if one flies from the water's edge for a moment, the chances are that it will return before long to the very same spot after a short, and no doubt successful, hunting expedition. In fact, because they tend to regard a particular reed or other favorite plant as home, you may find the very same one still there days later.

Dragonflies also have equally attractive relatives, which are known as damselflies. You can find out more about these other members of the family on pages 214-217. Both dragonflies and damselflies get their common names from their coloring or from the way in which they behave – for example, there are species generally known as the blue-tailed damselfly, the red-eyed damselfly, the white-faced darter, and the azure hawker. Each of these is depicted in the illustration shown here. Can you identify which is which?

World of the dragonfly

- Although all dragonflies have large jaws and nasty-looking pincers at the ends of their bodies, they are harmless to animals and humans. In fact, they are only dangerous to other insects, which they will regularly catch and consume in large quantities.

Carnivorous beauties

Belonging to an order of insects known as *Odonata*, meaning "toothed," dragonflies have biting mouthparts and strong mandibles – ideal for a carnivore. They also have good eyesight and a head that swivels, both of which are excellent tools for spotting prey.

Dragonflies are wonderful hunters. Because they fly so fast and are so acrobatic, they can even catch most other insects while still in the air.

Using their legs like a basket to trap their prey, they will take a larger insect back to a favorite perch and then devour it there.

The larger dragonflies may even swoop down over water to snatch a small frog or fish. The dragonfly shown here has caught a small Dobsonfly. All dragonflies are, of course, carnivores, so that they only eat other living creatures and never plants.

FACTFILE

In spite of their delicate looks, dragonflies are keen hunters, seizing and killing insects very adeptly, even in mid-air.

When a dragonfly has hatched from its egg as a nymph and starts to live under the water, it eats enormous amounts of food. Anything – such as other insect larvae, water lice, worms, tadpoles and small fish – that happens to come within range will be snapped up in its powerful jaws.

MASKED MONSTER

The dragonfly nymph has a very strange lip, known as a mask, under its chin. This provides a perfect insect trap and is like a large hand with a pair of pincers, at the end of a long arm. When the nymph is resting, the mask cannot be seen. But if the nymph spots a possible victim, out shoots the mask and the unfortunate passing insect will be seized by the pincers and greedily devoured. The nymph is a dull brown color and well camouflaged, so it is rarely detected in time.

Once a dragonfly nymph emerges from its watery home and splits out of its skin, however, it is in great danger. Unable to fly for an hour or two, it is at risk itself from being eaten by spiders, fish, or water birds.

Many birds would like to make a meal of an adult dragonfly but few are swift and agile enough. The exception is one called a hobby. A type of falcon, this bird of prey can fly much faster than dragonflies and will hunt them down, catching them in the air.

Water bugs

There are a number of true bugs that are able to perform the most remarkable feats in a watery environment.

Who would have thought that, miracles aside, it is possible to walk on water! Well, believe it or not, there are a few true bugs that can actually do this. Among them is the pond-skater, shown in the illustration *below*. It skims gracefully over the water surface in a skillful fashion, and feeds on any insects that come its way. Extremely sensitive to vibrations, it becomes aware very easily of the presence of potential prey and skates along to try to capture it. The pond-skater inserts its mouthparts into the victim and sucks up its insides. There are sea-skaters, too, that can be found skating over a deep ocean surface, possibly many hundreds of miles away from the nearest landmass.

UPSIDE-DOWN

One particular type of true water bug, known as a backswimmer, does precisely that; it propels itself along *upside-down*, its wing covers helping it glide through the water just below the

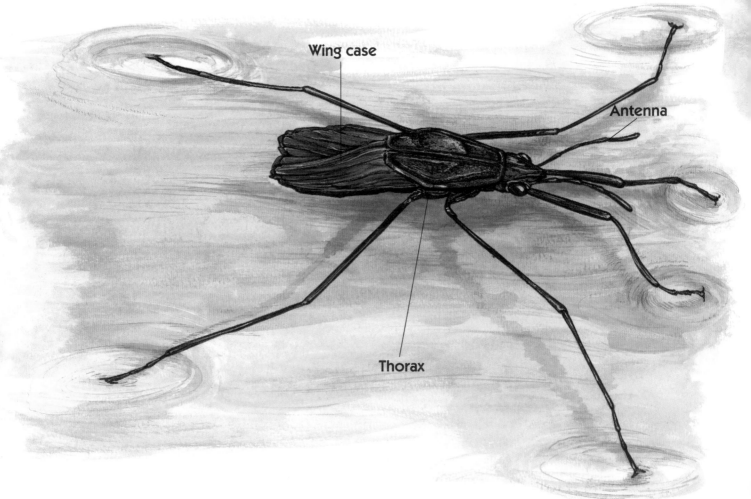

Wing case

Antenna

Thorax

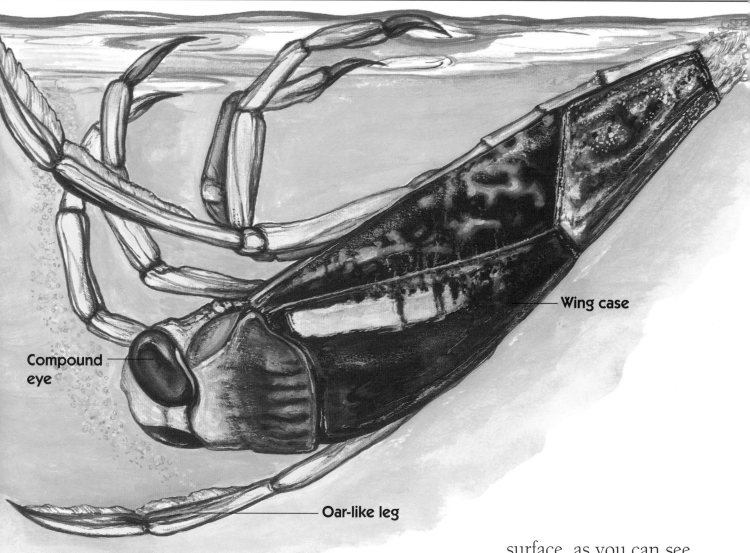

Compound eye

Wing case

Oar-like leg

World of the water bug

- The saucer bug lives in muddy ponds. It has a large, round body and comes to the surface every now and then for air. Shore bugs, meanwhile, are frequently found in a cleaner environment, near the water's edge.

surface, as you can see *above*. It, too, is predatory. In fact, it is among the most ferocious of all the water bugs. So be wary of keeping any in an aquarium with small fish, or tadpoles. Any backswimmers would certainly devour these and maybe bite you, too! Interestingly, their stance while swimming seems to be controlled by light. In fact, scientists have found that if backswimmers are placed in a tank that is lit from below, not above, they start to swim the right-way up, instead of on their backs.

Underwater worms

Next time you are near the sea coast, a lake, or a river, see if you can spot any of the strange-looking worms that live in the water.

Not all worms live in the soil. Many live where they are rarely seen by humans – beneath the water.

Bristleworms, for instance, which usually live in the ocean, look very different from earthworms, as you can

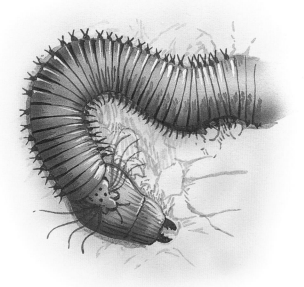

A number of underwater worms build defenses around themselves that act like houses and provide protection. Tube worms, *above*, for example, live on coral reefs in tubes they make themselves from lime.

The sand mason worms, *below*, meanwhile, are named because of their habit of making a home from sand and bits of shell. As you can see, they are very good at this.

see in the picture *above*. Like fish and some kinds of snails, they have lots of gills which they use for breathing under water, and pairs of paddles attached to the bristles help them swim. Many also have eyes and feelers. Unlike earthworms, too, most types of bristleworm are not hermaphrodites but either male or female, and some of them will sting.

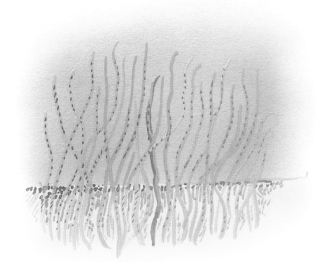

World of the underwater worm

- Some types of wriggly seaworms, found among coral reefs, are eaten by people of the Pacific region. But we do not suggest you try them.

Tubifex worms, shown *above*, also live in tubes. These peculiar creatures burrow into mud at the bottom of the water and live upside-down, their heads always in the mud searching for food.

If you have ever visited the beach, you may have seen evidence of lugworms, like those *below*. These creatures live in burrows under the sand, which they swallow, taking nourishment from minute particles. When the lugworm

has passed through them, the grains of sand form a mound known as a cast. Before long, these mounds build up and form distinctive little clumps all over the beach. Near the mounds, you will usually find a small hole, which is the entrance to the lugworm's burrow.

Ribbon worms, meanwhile, like the one *above*, also live by the sea in sand or mud. They can be very long when stretched out – up to the length of a basketball court, in fact.

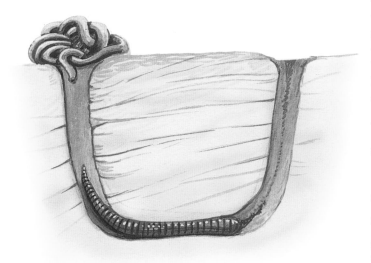

Leeches

Not very attractive creatures, leeches are greedy, but their appetite for blood does, in fact, have important uses.

Worms are generally considered to be harmless creatures. But the leech, a close relative of the earthworm, is in fact a dangerous, bloodsucking hunter.

Most leeches live in ponds, rivers, and streams. Excellent swimmers, they will loop their bodies through the water, as shown *below left*, until they find a likely-looking victim – a fish or a frog, for example. But they can also get around on land, moving in much the same way as caterpillars do.

Unlike earthworms, leeches do not have bristles on their bodies. Instead, they have two suckers – a small one at the front around the mouth and one at the back of their bodies. They will use these to attach themselves to a victim, such as the fish you can see *below*. Then they inject a chemical that stops the blood clotting, and start sucking.

Some leeches like nothing better than to swallow earthworms whole. And

when feeding on small insects or snails, leeches will often suck out their entire insides for a meal, as in the illustration *below right*.

BLOODSUCKERS

Long ago, it was common for doctors to place a special type of leech on the flesh of their patients. With its three sets of teeth, it would keep sucking blood until it had filled itself up. At the time, doctors thought that having some blood sucked out in this way would help the sick to get well. But it was not really helpful at all in curing disease.

However, leeches are of use in one special form of medicine today. This is microsurgery where, for example, a surgeon may have to sew someone's finger back into position after it has been severed in an accident.

If the surgeon attaches a leech to the finger for about twenty minutes after it has been sewn back, the blood will flow easily, and this will help the veins in the finger work normally again.

The leech has a substance in its saliva that stops the blood from clotting for several hours, even after the leech has been removed. So leeches can be helpful after such an operation.

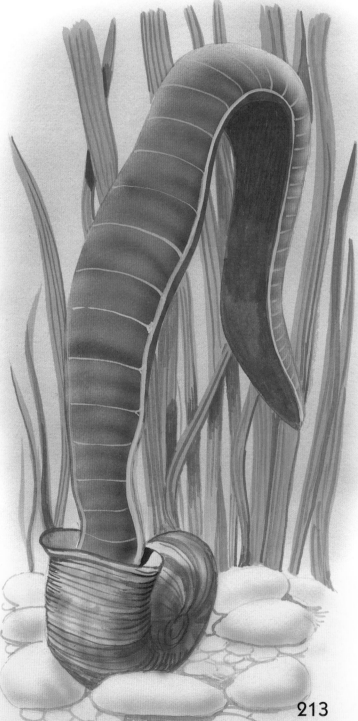

World of the leech

- Leeches have rows of tiny, sharp teeth on their suckers, which are used to bite through the skin of a victim, so the leech can get to the blood supply.

Damselflies

Smaller in general than their relatives, the dragonflies, these insects are exquisitely beautiful, too.

Never wandering far from the water in which they breed, damselflies love any watery environment that has copious supplies of aquatic plants on which they can rest.

Thorax

Antenna

Compound eye

From the specimen shown here, you can see what attractive creatures they are. With wings that are sometimes colored blue, red, or green, if you watch them closely, you will see that damselflies tend to flutter rather than fly or dart around like dragonflies do. Their wings may be long, but the muscles that operate the flight mechanism are not so strong. If you have a chance, see if you can spot them when they are resting, too. They hold their wings erect over their backs,

as butterflies do; or, alternatively, they have them partly spread out. Dragonflies, on the other hand, always rest with their wings outspread.

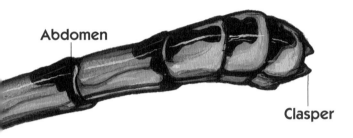

Abdomen

Clasper

HOVERING HUNTERS

In spite of being weak fliers, damselflies are nevertheless good hunters, even on the wing; and some species will greedily catch midges while fluttering in the air. Others have been known to hover near a spider's web; and if they spot a victim entrapped there, they will attempt to steal it for a meal – without becoming tangled themselves.

The larvae, too, are very greedy, and have strange mouthparts. The lower jaw is like a pair of pincers and can be pushed forward to scratch prey. When not in use, however, these pincers lie under the chin.

Although generally smaller than dragonflies, the very biggest damselflies are, in fact, larger than the biggest dragonflies. Unlike dragonflies, too, damselflies have four wings that tend to be about the same size: the front wings of dragonflies, however, are usually larger than their hind wings.

Damselflies also have eyes that are set more widely apart than those of dragonflies and do not usually join in the middle. Their narrow necks turn very easily – most useful for spotting potential predators, of course. But dragonflies, as shown on pages 198-207, have bigger eyes that provide a much more generous vista for them, without the need to turn their heads.

KEEPING CLEAN

Damselflies are often thought of as being fastidious insects because of the way they have been spotted cleaning their eyes and antennae with their front legs. They will even sometimes use their back legs to clean the end of their abdomens.

Turn now and discover how the males and females of some types of damselflies perform an elegant courtship ritual and then get down to the process of mating.

World of the damselfly

- In tropical America, a legend grew that, if you find a large damselfly with wings that are transparent and ghost-like, and with only the colored tips visible, it is the spirit of someone who has recently died.

Getting together

Female's wing

The aim is for the female's body to permit entry by the male's sperm. They remain in this position for a while, and the female will then lay her fertilized eggs on a water plant or in the water itself.

IN TANDEM
The male is highly chivalrous. He actually helps his mate get out of the water safely after she has laid the eggs, by hauling her up. During this activity, it sometimes looks as if they are harnessed together.

When a male spreads his wings, he may be signaling to a passing female damselfly. Let mating begin!

Facing the female, the male damselfly starts to flutter to and fro. He is engaging in an elaborate

Female's abdmen

courtship dance – very entertaining to watch. It will not be long before they actually mate while resting on a stem or twig, as in this illustration, shown *above*. The male takes hold of the female with his clasper, and both insects start to twist their bodies.

Male's wing

They may even fly around in tandem in this way for a while.

WATERY HABITAT

The emerging larvae – also known as nymphs – will, in fact, spend all their lives in the water and shed their skin from time to time. As yet, they have no wings; and they are able to breathe through three tiny external gills, as well as through their skin.

It will take a year – sometimes much longer – for the larvae to mature. Then, they will leave the water by climbing up a reed. Soon, their skin starts to split and the adult damselfly emerges in much the same way as a dragonfly is born. It is colorless and soft at first, but the wings will soon harden and the damselfly takes on a glittering hue. It will then take to the air, even though not as confidently as a dragonfly. It may even be that, within a day or so, it finds a mate of its own, and the whole damselfly cycle can begin once more.

Male's reproductive opening

FACTFILE

Some males will stay with the female until she drops her eggs. They do this in order to prevent any rival males from approaching.

217

Water spiders

It is common to find spiders lurking in the bathtub. But did you know that some types of spiders actually spend most of their lives under water?

Next time you pass a pond of still water, try some detective work. See if there are any little splashes which seem to show that something has come to the surface. You could be looking at evidence that a special type of spider is alive and well, and has made its home in the middle of the pond!

These underwater spiders have to come up for air from time to time, but generally hide under water to ambush their prey.

Some underwater spiders are also known as fishing spiders. Quite large, they sometimes grab tiny fish and feast on them if they get too hungry while waiting for a passing insect.

Be sure not to handle underwater spiders, however, because they can give you a poisonous bite.

The water spider has come up with a clever plan for a ready underwater air

World of water spiders

- If you spot a spider in your bathtub, it is not a true water spider, but one that lost its footing and fell into the bathtub, or it could have been wafted in through the window. Rescue it, because this type of spider cannot swim.

supply. It first spins its web, which lies flat just underneath the surface of the pond. Then it swims up to the top and traps a bubble of air between its back legs, as shown in the picture on the page *opposite*.

Very carefully, it brings the bubble under the web by climbing down water plants. The spider might have to do this hundreds of times until the air has stretched the web into a kind of thimble shape, as shown *below*. Now, the spider can live comfortably under water, waiting to trap insects for its daily meal.

The under water spider also thinks ahead. The special water thimble will hold enough air for about 4-5 months. This means it can survive under water for the whole winter season.

GOOD VIBRATIONS

Water spiders are so sensitive to vibrations that they can readily detect any insect activity on the surface. When alerted in this way, they will leave their thimble and pounce on the victim, grasping it with their legs before bringing it toward their fangs. Fishing spiders, meanwhile, sit on floating leaves and dash out to catch passing prey. But the sheet web that a water spider spins, complete with thimble, is not for catching prey. Instead, it provides a resting place only.

FACTFILE

Water spiders hunt mostly at night but they always return to their homes to feed on what they catch, rather than eating it right away.

Water snails

Freshwater snails are generally harmless. But some that live in the sea are highly poisonous, so you have to watch out!

All snails like damp places to set up house in, but over three-quarters of all species of snails actually live in water their entire lives. They can be found in ponds, rock pools, babbling brooks, mighty rivers, cool streams or deep blue lakes, anywhere in the world.

Most snails are air-breathers and come up for gulps; but some stay underwater all the time, breathing the air in the water. Some may even have gills, like fish. They often lurk at the bottom, out of the way, so that it is difficult to find them.

Other snails are quite a bit bolder. They live just underneath the surface, perhaps floating upside-down. They will feed, like the snail you can see in the illustration *below*, on the slimy green blanket, made up of algae, which often covers the surface of ponds.

Freshwater snails do not mind how cold the water gets, as long as it does not freeze. In sunny weather, however, they will hide under rocks and in deep crevices to escape the heat. Some types of snails, such as the marsh snail, are even happy living in the dirty, smelly water of stagnant ponds.

Some sea snails, meanwhile, can be killers – the cone shell, for example. It rests by day but comes out at night to hunt and feed on worms, other mollusks, and fish that it can sniff out.

World of water snails

- Many water snails have gills that allow them to breathe under the water and stay down for some time, although they will also come to the surface for air.

The sea snail then stabs the prey with its venomous tongue. It can even poison humans.

Diving beetles

Wing
case

Swimming
legs

Compound
eye

Grasping
leg

Antenna

How terrifying
it must be for
a diving
beetle's tiny prey
to face the
fearsome-looking
creature swimming
toward it!

Varying in
length from
0.8-1.5in
(2-38mm),
diving beetles
are oval-shaped and usually dark green-
black in color, with touches of yellow.

They need their hairy hind legs
for swimming, and these are used
rather like a pair of oars to speed
the diving beetle along.

Diving beetles have wings and can
take to the air. However, they spend
most of their time in the water,
where they continually prey on
insects and tadpoles. They may even go
after tiny frogs and sticklebacks. In fact,
you are likely to find them in any still
pond where there are waterweeds

World of the diving beetle

- It is easy to tell a male and female diving beetle apart. Look for grooves running the length of the wing-cases in a female. These are smoother, however, in a male diving beetle.

- Never keep diving beetles in an aquarium, because they may attack your fish. Amazingly, their larvae are even more greedy than the adults, and highly ferocious, too.

because, from time to time, they come to the surface of the water to breathe, and then dive back down again – hence their name. They will store air under their wing covers to ensure a supply underwater.

WATER TIGERS

Mating between diving beetles usually takes place in spring, and the females will lay their eggs, not on the surface of the water, but on a reed or water plant stem. The larvae that eventually emerge are exceedingly ferocious, in spite of their very small size, and are sometimes called water tigers because of their predatory behavior.

Diving beetle larvae look a lot different from the adults – rather like scorpions, in fact. But, unlike their land-dwelling lookalikes, they can swim and also like to walk along the bottom of the water.

When these larvae have trapped their prey, they do not swallow it whole. Instead, using special digestive juices, they turn their victim's body into a liquid, which is then sucked up. All that remains is a husk.

By the time they become adults, however, diving beetles give up sucking their victims dry in this way. Instead. they now start to chew at their meals with the very strong jaws that they develop in maturity.

NASTY LITTLE SQUIRTS

Their strong jaws also serve as fighting tools when adult diving beetles are attacked. But these curious creatures also have another weapon in their armory of defense against predators. They are able to squirt white liquid, which has an extremely nasty odor, from their thoraxes in the direction of their enemies, in the attempt to keep them at bay.

FACTFILE

The diving beetle may attack if handled, and it has been known to turn cannibalistic if there is nothing else around to eat.

Gallery of bugs

Bugs vary so much in their behavior and appearance that it is possible to divide them into a whole range of categories.

As you study this section of the encyclopedia, you will gradually become familiar with over sixty different bugs that have marked personality traits. Some, for example, are superb athletes for their body size, running at spectacular rates or leaping to tremendous heights or great lengths. There are many that fully deserve to come under the heading of assassins, so deadly are they when face-to-face with their prey. And there are others that attract a mate, or deter an enemy, by giving off all sorts of aromas, some highly disgusting, others much more pleasant.

Many bugs are master builders, constructing wonderful dwellings for themselves or even whole colonies for their community. Some sing superbly, providing open-air concerts. Carers, sparklers, scavengers, and others – all are featured, too. Time, now, to get wise to the principal characteristics of some of the most fantastic creepy-crawlies inhabiting our planet.

Aviators

Some bugs that fly always cruise along at a very gentle speed. Others, however, dart through the air with quick energy, and could be called the jet craft of the world of bugs.

Butterflies are spectacular aviators. Some will even migrate in large numbers over huge distances. Locusts, too, migrate but are, of course, a much less welcome sight. The ordinary housefly, meanwhile, should not be overlooked for its skills in the air. In fact, it has powerful wings and may beat them at the mind-blowing rate of 200 times per second if trying to escape a predator. There are even some bugs that will secretly hitch a free ride from a flying insect – the larva of the blister beetle, for instance, will ride on the back of a bee. What a sneaky stowaway this bug is!

Ladybugs
A type of beetle, the **ladybug** has strong wings for its tiny size and is known to travel in large swarms in search of greenflies.

Monarch butterflies
Migrating long distances to warmer climes – from Canada to California in winter, for example – **Monarchs** nevertheless have only a 3-4in (7.5-10cm) wingspan.

226

Bees

A **bumblebee** is a skilled aviator and can beat its wings very rapidly. But the speed at which it moves is far surpassed by the hover-fly, shown *below left*.

Lacewings

Fluttering is a main characteristic of the **lacewing**. It does not fly great distances, but it moves very delicately when in the air.

Hover flies

True to its name, the **hover fly** can hover in mid-air; and, in doing so, moves its wings at the most phenomenal rate of about 1,000 beats per second.

Builders

Some bugs construct the most extraordinary, many-chambered homes for their colonies – under or on the ground, or in the treetops. The materials they use are varied – leaves, earth, mud, silk, twigs, straw, and also woodpulp.

Certain ants literally sew themselves into a home, producing a shelter that can hang from a tree. Others, however, take up residence underground. Termites, meanwhile, build the most bizarre towers imaginable. These structures may take several years to complete and end up as tall as giraffes. What is more, inside each of these marvelous mounds there could be as many as several million termite residents that originated from a single king and queen. Several more strange edifices built by bugs are illustrated here.

Weaver ants

This type of **ant** uses silk produced by its larvae to sew together a whole series of leaves into a bulky shape that provides an excellent protective structure for them.

Mud-dauber wasps

This type of **wasp** often builds its nest in human homes. It looks like a lump of clay and is bigger than an adult man's fist when finished. It is really a cluster of cells for future offspring, plastered with lots of mud and with splashes for camouflage.

Termites

The nests built by these master architects come in a wide range of shapes and sizes. Some look like mushrooms; others have a wigwam shape; still others are constructed as rounded shapes in trees. **Termite** mounds are made from spit, earth, and droppings.

Froghoppers

In order to hide from predators, a **froghopper** will whip up the plant sap that it has been sucking and seek shelter right inside the bubbly froth.

House spiders

With webs not nearly as evenly structured webs as those of the orb spider, house spiders build sheet-webs, or cobwebs, for the same purpose – to catch prey.

Athletes

Not all bugs are like snails that crawl along at a slow pace. Some can, in fact, run very quickly, while others may be strong jumpers or hoppers.

Tree hoppers
Looking much like part of the stem on which it has been sitting, a **tree hopper** may suddenly kick out its back legs, and the strong muscles in its thorax will propel it into the air.

Grasshoppers
The **grasshopper** excels at catapulting itself along, which it does by using a spring mechanism in its knees. It can also use its wings to fly.

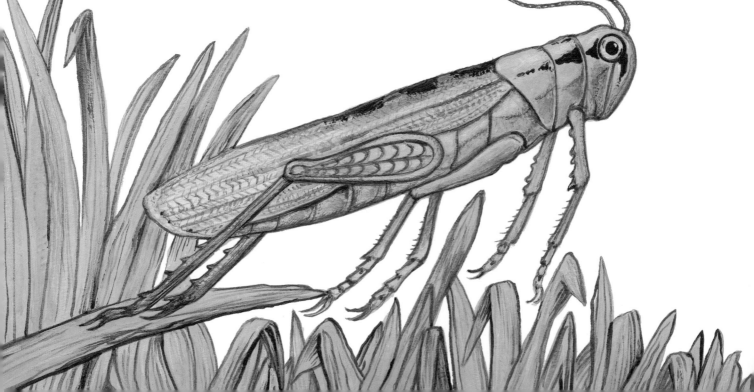

Not all apparently athletic bugs are powered by strong legs or a substance like resilin, which gives fleas their spring. A certain pond beetle, for example, has an intriguing way of escaping from predators. When an enemy is in sight, the beetle automatically releases a chemical from its abdomen, and this floats to the surface of the water. The chemical then expands so rapidly that it propels the beetle along at a speedy rate. The world of bugs is certainly full of the most fantastic marathon runners, jumpers, and even hoppers!

Springtails

If this agile little bug suddenly straightens its two-pronged tail, it is able to propel itself high into the air – thus its highly descriptive name.

Click beetles

In a single leap, a **click beetle** – if it finds itself upside down after falling on its back – will throw itself as high as 1ft (30cm) into the air and straighten its stance to the sound of a click.

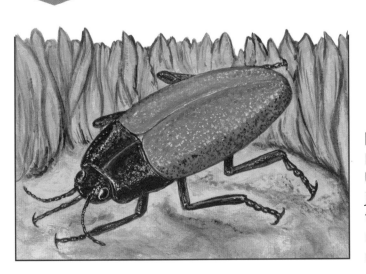

Fleas

It may be hard to believe but these remarkable high-jumpers can propel themselves with a force many times greater than that required to launch a rocket into space!

Tricksters

Lots of bugs are crafty in their own way – instinctively, not by choice. Some, for instance, look just like the vegetation surrounding them and so are well camouflaged.

Normally harmless-looking because of its exquisite and fragile beauty, a certain butterfly from India will rest on a branch and, if approached by a predator, will take on the stance of a highly poisonous snake. Other bugs, therefore, steer clear of it. Bright coloring also sometimes presents a

Hover flies
With almost identical coloring and form, these flies are superb bee mimics. All they lack is the bee's sting.

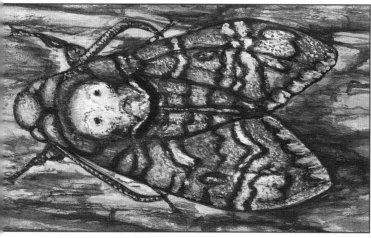

Death's head Hawkmoths
This type of **Hawkmoth** has markings on its head that closely resemble a human skull. It can also shriek just like a mouse at times, completely confusing a predator.

Trapdoor spiders
This very crafty creature hides in its burrow and makes a hinged trapdoor through which its next meal will fall. The **trapdoor spider** is then ready to pounce.

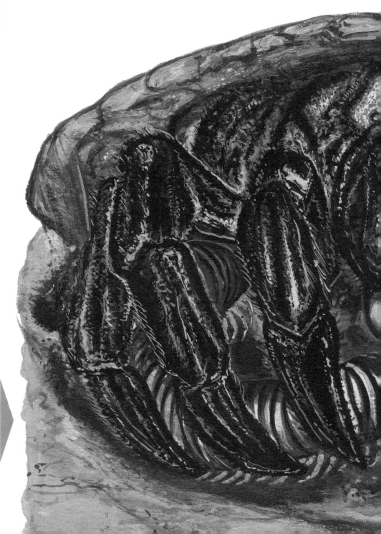

warning to a predator, as will a nasty taste. Once it has a mouthful of something disgusting, the enemy will not bother with that sort of prey again. All the bugs featured here are talented tricksters in different ways, and each is able to double-cross a predator with the aim of self-preservation – either by its appearance or by some sort of fatal trap.

Leaf insects

They look like old, dried-out leaves, in color and because they keep so still – hence, their name. Stick insects, meanwhile, with their long, thin bodies, closely resemble twigs and branches. Both types are extremely well camouflaged, fooling potential predators.

Thorn bugs

Next time you are near a rose bush, study it thoroughly. You may find that what you first thought was just another thorn is, in fact, a **thorn bug**, and alive!

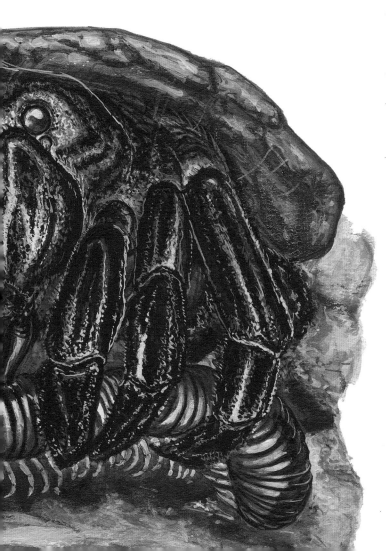

Stinkers

Some bugs may not have killer jaws or a deadly sting. They can, however, deter an enemy in another very effective way – by producing a very nasty smell.

Beware the bombardier beetle! If you disturb it, as you can see *below*, it will be ready to release a squirt of liquid that may not only cause you a slight burn; it will smell disgusting, too.

The scorpion-fly has a similar means of defense, using a foul yellow chemical that it produces. There are even so-called skunk-flies that are particularly true to their name (taken from the animal, the skunk, that is very well known for the powerful odors it emits).

Other bugs, though, use aromas not to deter enemies but to attract a mate. Certain ants, too, will exude a perfumed trail that others can follow – to a food source, perhaps. Smells have many important uses in the world of bugs.

Bombardier beetles
These reddish-brown beetles produce their very own stink bombs. They can release a boiling hot, smelly, smoke-like gas from their rear, if a predator threatens.

Butterflies

Lots of **butterflies** – both males and females – use their own distinctive perfumes as part of their courtship rituals. These aromas may also deter enemies that, in contrast, find them repulsive.

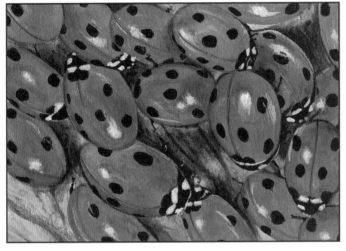

Stink bugs

Shield bugs are often called by the highly descriptive alternative name above because of the foul aromas they produce, thereby warding off creatures that might make a meal of them.

Ladybugs

Pretty as they are, **ladybugs** nevertheless give out a nasty stink if disturbed. No wonder they have few predators!

Cockroaches

It is often possible to tell that a kitchen has been infested by **cockroaches** because of the putrid smell they leave behind as their calling card.

Sparklers

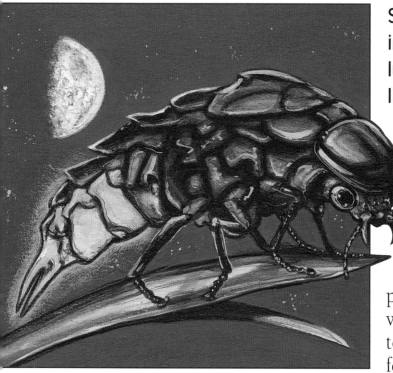

Some bugs have their own built-in irridescence and glow with a superb luster that makes them seem like living lanterns.

Female glowworms – and their eggs and larvae, too – shine so brilliantly that you could probably read by their light after sundown. The males therefore have no trouble in finding a mate. Certain centipedes are also luminous, particularly at the center of their bodies; while fireflies, true to their name, seem to carry flashlights that will illuminate a forest path at nightfall. In parts of the West Indies, it was once fashionable for ladies to wear fireflies in their hair, where they would sparkle like a diamond tiara. In the world of bugs, such brilliance can be a mating signal, but it may also lure unwary prey.

Glowworms
The female will display the luminous end of her body, in an attempt to lure the male to her. **Glowworm** larvae also light up if they are disturbed.

Railroad worms
By night, the larvae of a certain type of beetle, which are known as **railroad worms**, will suddenly glow red at their heads, while their bodies turn greenish yellow if attacked or when mating.

Firefly beetles

You may sometimes see them at night, flashing across the sky as they try to catch the eye of a mate. The **firefly beetle** has even been described as a living lantern, and was once kept in a tiny cage to light up primitive tropical homes.

Centipedes

Some species of **centipedes** glow in the dark, leaving behind irridescent slime, too, as they try to attract a mate. They need to do this sparingly, however, as it takes a month to become shiny again if all the luminosity is used up.

Musicians

You do not necessarily have to go to a party or attend an outdoor pop concert to hear music on a spring or summer evening.

While the males are silent, female mosquitoes buzz in monotonous fashion and sound like the sort of noise you, too, could make if you blow through a comb and paper. Grasshoppers are much more lively in their song, however, and so are katydids. But cicadas and crickets are counted among the most melodious of all. Certain scorpions, some spiders, and even a South American butterfly, make

Cicadas

Male **cicadas** are the star musical performers of the entire insect world. In some species, the level of sound produced to lure a mate may reach over 100 decibels.

Bush crickets

Also known as katydids because their song sounds just like this word, the long-horned **bush crickets** use their wing cases to make delightful music.

interesting sounds, too, even though you might think of them as silent types. Try listening out for a whole range of musical bugs. You may be rewarded by a splendidly rhythmic and tuneful recital. Some, though, will often chirp more slowly when it is chilly.

Musk beetles

When the **Musk beetle** moves long, it grates its neck against the next segment of its body, and this produces a sound comparable to that of a squeaking door that needs oiling.

Bumblebees

One of the most familiar musicians of the world of insects is undoubtedly the **bumblebee**, with its incessant buzz. Some bees even make sounds that have particular meanings for their fellow bees.

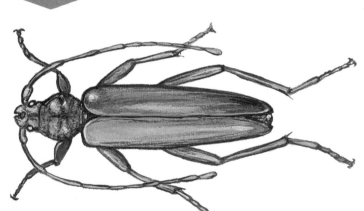

Tarantulas

If you find a knife and run it across the teeth of an ordinary hair comb, you will hear a sound that comes very close to that made by the large **tarantula** when it is taken by surprise.

Assassins

Praying mantis
Often described as a formidable killing machine, though not large by any means, the **praying mantis** can grab its prey – be it an insect or a small frog, or perhaps, in the case of a female, her mate – in a mere fraction of a second.

Although they are small, many bugs will be out for the kill if they come across a likely meal. And what fearsome assassins they can be!

Ants will frequently hunt down termites in particular parts of the world. But termites can go one better. They have very sharp jaws and, if attacked, will bite the enemy ants in half. Some may even explode, committing a sort of hari-kiri in order to spray any invading ants with a foul and deadly yellow matter.

The so-called assassin bug, meanwhile, is clever and will camouflage itself with termite feces. It then launches an attack, killing for a termite feast. Other bugs will poison, bite, or choke their victims to death in a hungry frenzy. Of course, the bugs that kill in this way will be carnivores, or perhaps omnivores. A few may even resort to cannibalism, eating their own kind if food supplies are very short. Those featured on these two pages are extremely savage beasts.

Robber flies

Watch out! An assassin is around!
With superb sight and quick
reactions, **robber flies** can catch
and kill insects, such as wasps,
that have stingers without being
attacked themselves.

Assassin bugs

Highly predatory, as their name clearly suggests,
assasin bugs will kill other insects at any opportunity,
using mouthparts that both pierce and suck, so that
they can feed on their victims' body fluids.

Wind scorpions

Highly aggressive, the **wind scorpion**
will rear up at an enemy and open its
gigantic jaws. It is a ferocious
carnivore, too, and will suck
its victims dry.

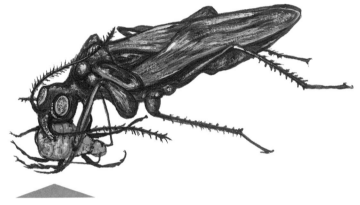

Miners

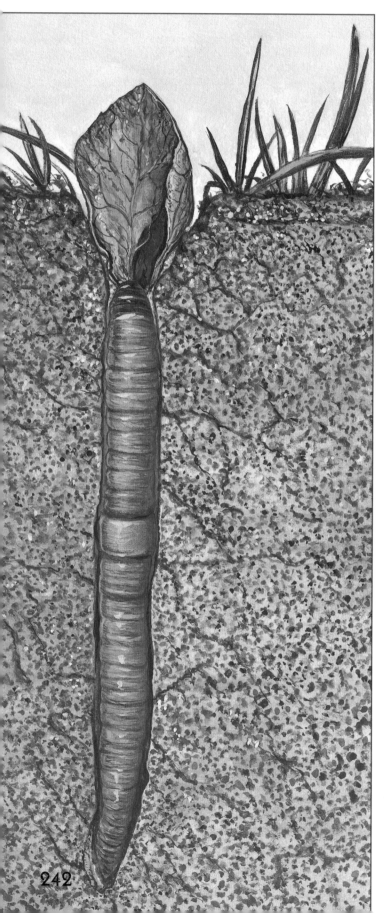

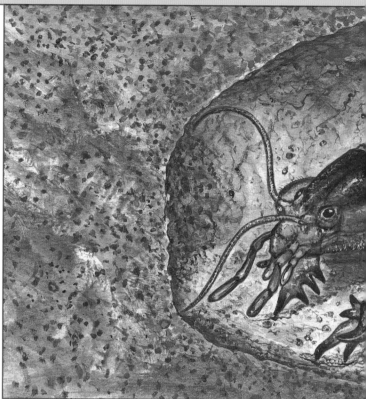

Many bugs like the underground life and burrow deep down into the earth. Others, meanwhile, drill into the surface of a tree or plant in order to deposit their eggs within the vegetation.

The mason wasp is a particularly skilled miner and will loosen the soil, into which it digs a tunnel by producing a liquid with special softening properties. This hard-working wasp will even

Earthworms
Worms are fantastic diggers and will also drag leaves into the shafts that they make for use as a food supply. They swallow the earth as they burrow, and then leave it as a cast on the surface.

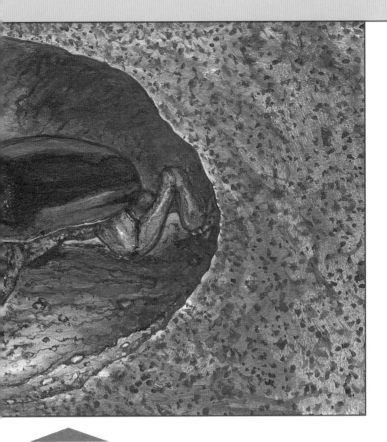

Mole crickets
Champion miners, **mole crickets** use their front claws as spades and also gnaw at any plant roots that get in the way. Their aim is to feed on the larvae of other bugs that live underground.

recycle the sand that it digs out, using it to close up its burrow when the tunnel has been constructed.

Some bees are also able to dig underground shafts, and ant-lions will excavate funnel-shaped pits in order to trap victims which they then suck dry. The Sexton beetle, too, goes underground to bury all manner of small creatures that it finds. Humans are certainly not alone in mining Planet Earth.

Sawflies
The female **sawfly** has an especially adapted part of its body for drilling holes in plants and trees. Here, she will lay her eggs. Her tool is her ovipositor, with sharp tips to its two blades.

Leaf-mining caterpillars
The **caterpillars** of this sort of moth are excellent at digging tunnels – not on the ground but on leaves. You can sometimes see the result of their activities on the surface of a plant.

Bloodsuckers

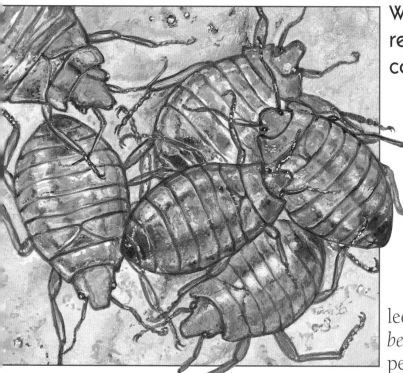

Bed bugs
Only about 0.15-0.35in (4-8mm) long, these tiny
iinsects feed on human blood at night, if given the
chance. In fact, if the female bites you, she will
swell to twice her size. Clean bedding is an
essential preventive.

Who would have thought that a relative of the gentle earthworm could be so bloodthirsty!

Water-dwelling leeches like nothing
more than a good meal of animal
blood – including yours. They
may even drink several times
their own body weight before
they have had enough; and such
a feast will provide them with
enough nourishment for weeks. In
fact, blood is all they ever eat. Some
leeches though, as you will discover
below, actually have medicinal uses, so
perhaps we should not dismiss them as
complete undesirables.

Several other types of creepy-crawlies –
among them bugs that also spread
disease when they bite – are always
hungry for blood, too. We may be giants
in comparison, but they still dare to
bite. Study these two pages, if you
dare, and meet some of the
most vicious.

Deer keds

These greedy little bloodsuckers are adept at climbing up a stem of grass so that they can bite a grazing deer. They don't just attack deer but horses, cattle or sheep, too.

Horse flies

If you have ever been attacked by a **horse fly**, it was a female that was to blame. Males feed on nectar, but the females like blood. With mouthparts like those of a mosquito, they can inflict a painful bite.

Leeches

These creatures love blood and may even be used in microsurgery to help circulation after an operation, so that there is less risk of a dangerous clot forming.

Scavengers

Have you ever wondered why we see so few dead birds, mice, or squirrels, even in the countryside? What happens to these creatures when they die?

Some carnivorous bugs are masters at the art of scavenging, and will either chew away at dead flesh or remove pieces to take to their colonies, so that their fellow bugs or offspring may feast. They do not kill for a meal but still enjoy eating meat.

Most scavenging bugs will eat on the go, wherever they find rotting flesh. Sexton beetles, however, like to dine in a more relaxed way. That is why, instead of scavenging on the spot, a pair will bury the carcass of any small animal that they find and then feed later. Sometimes, the female will even see the male on his way after mating so that she has most of the feast to herself.

Sexton beetles
These undertakers of the bug world bury birds and other creatures in order to feast. They also lay their eggs on them, so that there is a ready food supply for the larvae.

Wood ants

Worker **wood ants** are socially minded scavengers. They are not merely opportunists that think just of themselves if they find a dead creature, but will carry back scraps to their nest so that the colony can feast, too.

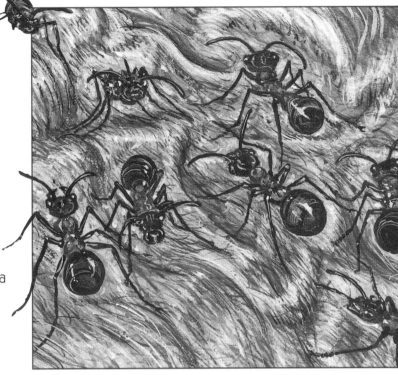

Snails

If **snails** come across a carcass, they tend to wait until other scavengers have had their fill of flesh and then nibble at any exposed bones. It is as if they know, instinctively, that the calcium that the bones contain will be good for their shells.

Scorpion-flies

Not only do they feed off dead creatures, but male **scorpion-flies** may also offer an insect corpse to females as a gift, prior to mating. At times they may even steal this from a spider's web in the attempt to please their partner.

Victims of plants

Some plants have developed ingenious ways of obtaining more nourishment. They act as death traps for the small creatures on which they like to feed!

Venus flytraps
This carnivorous plant originates from eastern North America. It has two lobes that will snap shut with tremendous speed if its hairs are touched, trapping a victim.

Bladderworts
There is no getting free when these underwater plants operate the trapdoors on their leaves. These will open, suck in a water-borne victim, and then close tight.

Trumpet pitcher plants

Flies and other insects are often attracted to a **pitcher plant** by its scent, only to fall inside, drowning in its juices and then decomposing so that the plant can feed on them.

In general, plants are able to obtain all the nutrients they need from soil, sunlight, air, and water. Yet many need additional nourishment too, and, to this end, they catch and devour bugs!

Carnivorous plants set traps for their unsuspecting victims. Their brightly colored leaves lure passing insects, as does their sweet-smelling nectar. Then, when the insect lands, it either becomes stuck or the plant's leaves trap it by slamming shut. The plant's insect meal is then broken down by special juices to aid digestion.

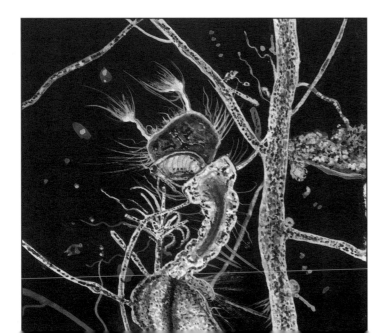

Sundew plants

Insects are lured by the sticky substance on these plants' long hairs, only to become stuck. The **sundew** stem then curls right around them, forming a powerful trap.

Caregivers

Some bugs make poor parents, never taking any interest at all in the future generation after the female has laid her eggs. Others, though, are much more conscientious.

The pregnant earwig makes careful preparation for her brood, digging a burrow in the soil where she can deposit her eggs, and then staying close by. Once her babies hatch, she will continue to take care of them and knows instinctively when it is time to let them cope for themselves.

Other bugs – certain wasps, for example – make sure their larvae have a ready food supply as soon as they hatch by laying their eggs inside aphids. Who would have thought that some spiders, and even a certain species of cockroach, would be excellent parents, too!

Cockroaches

Not generally maternal, the females of one type of **cockroach**, unlike others, make excellent parents and will carry their larvae around with them, safely tucked up under their abdomen, for a while.

Worker ants

These are among the most hard-working of all insects. They play an important part in their society by building a nest, helping to run it, too, and foraging for food for the queen ant and all her brood.

Shield bugs

These small insects have a strong maternal instinct, protecting their many nymphs from any marauding predators while they feed greedily during this important growth stage.

Fungus beetles

Many insects desert their young; but the female **fungus beetle** is very loyal to her brood. She guards her eggs and helps the larvae find food.

Nursery web spider

This exemplary mother will spin a covering of silk over her egg sac, which has been deposited on a leaf, and then guard it with her life until the young hatch.

Infesters

Lots of bugs cause damage to our crops, and even to our homes, if they infest. Pesticides may be needed at times to eradicate them; but there may be other preferable ways of coping with these persistent mini-beasts, too.

Fire ants are hungry bugs. They feed on other insects but also often eat plants that have only just started to sprout. No wonder, then, that they are cursed by farmers if they infest a field. Sometimes, though, use of insecticides can do harm to other creatures, not only directly but also by depriving them of the bugs on which they previously fed.

A better approach, therefore, in instances of aphid infestation, for example, is the introduction of ladybugs that will feast on them. There are other insects, too, that may help with the elimination of certain pests. The chalcid wasp, for instance, can be useful, as described *below*. The biological control of insect pests is no easy matter.

Whiteflies

They may look like harmless snowflakes; but these tiny bugs are related to aphids and are dreadful pests. They will infest tropical crops by sucking at their sap. **Whiteflies** can be controlled by the chalcid wasp, however.

Silverfish

If you spot these 0.4in (1cm)-long bugs, it could be that your home is damp. Most often, they lurk among old papers.

Colarado potato beetles

These striped bugs will feed on potato leaves both as larvae and as adults, so the tubers do not develop and the harvest is ruined.

Cabbage white caterpillars

Caterpillars of the cabbage white butterfly, as their name suggests, love cabbage leaves. There could not be a more unwelcome sight to farmers who grow this crop.

Glossary

aestivation – passing the summer in a state of rest

algae – plants without true stems, roots or leaves, living in moist conditions

antennae – feelers

antihistamine – a drug to treat an allergy

apiarist – a bee-keeper

apiary – a hive

arachnid – a type of arthropod with four pairs of legs, such as a spider or scorpion

arthropod – any small creature with jointed limbs and a hard exoskeleton

bee-bread – a mixture of honey and pollen

cannibals – creatures that eat their own kind

carnivores – meat-eaters

casts – the feces of worms

chrysalis – a pupa (plural, *pupae*)

cocoon – a silk protective casing in which pupae develop

compound eyes – eyes with many lenses

crop – a bee's special stomach for storing nectar

diurnal – coming out by day

drones – male bees

echolocation – finding an object by measuring the time it takes for an echo to return

elytra – wing cases

entomologist – an expert on bugs

entomology – the study of bugs

epiphragm – a mucus plug produced by snails

exoskeleton – an outer casing, enclosing soft body parts

feces – waste matter

gills – breathing organs

grubs – the young of various bugs

hibernate – to rest during the winter

host – a creature or plant, off which another creature lives

honeydew – a substance made by aphids

hybrids – an animal or plant resulting from a cross between two genetically different animals or plants

imago – the early mature stage of an insect

insect – a small air-breathing arthropod with three pairs of legs, usually two pairs of wings, and a head, thorax and abdomen

insectivores – creatures that eat insects

larva – the young of bugs that undergo a complete metamorphosis

mandibles – a bug's jaws or mouthparts

maxillae – mouthparts in arthropods

meconium – waste matter

mimicry – looking or behaving like another creature

molt – to lose an outer covering

nacre – mother-of-pearl

nectar – a sugary fluid collected by bees from flowers

nocturnal – coming out by night

nymphs – the young of certain bugs that do not undergo complete metamorphosis

ootheca – the purse in which a cockroach carries her eggs

operculum – an opening in the shells of some snails

palps –feelers

parthenogenetic – reproducing without fertilization of eggs

petide – an ant's waist section

pedipalps – appendages in arachnids

pheromones – chemicals secreted by bugs that affect their behavior

pollen – a substance produced by seed-bearing plants and necessary for their reproduction

pollination – the fertilization of a plant

proboscis – elongated mouthparts or type of tongue

propolis – resinous substance collected by bees from trees

pupae –the young of bugs that undergo a complete metamorphosis

protozoa – very primitive, tiny life forms

quinine – a medicinal drug

regurgitate – to bring up again

royal jelly –a substance secreted by worker bees

saddle – the pink central part of a worm

saliva – secretions from the mouth

stridulation – the making of sound by an insect as it rubs one part of its body against another part

symbiotic – with a close, interdependent relationship

tegmina – forewings of the cockroach and related insects

terrarium – a container in which to keep bugs or other small creatures, or plants

ultra-sonic sounds – sounds that are beyond our normal hearing range

viviparous –giving birth to live offspring

Index

Index